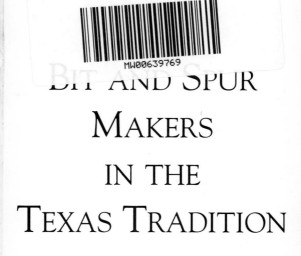

BIT AND SPUR
MAKERS
IN THE
TEXAS TRADITION

POCKET GUIDE

NED AND JODY MARTIN AND KURT HOUSE

PUBLISHED BY HAWK HILL PRESS

ISBN: 0-9659947-3-2

Design and printing by Printing Partners
103 E. Lemon Avenue, Suite 219
Monrovia, California 91016

Hawk Hill Press
P. O. Box 555, Nicasio, CA 94946
1-888-462-2390
www.hawkhillpress.com

TABLE OF CONTENTS

Valuing Bits and Spurs

Based on a more complete discussion of the subject by Bruce and Julianne Bartlett in the hardbound edition of *Bit and Spur Makers in the Texas Tradition.*

Criteria to be considered when valuing antique bits and spurs:

- ➤ Recent auction results
  - See catalogs
- ➤ Comparable private sales
- ➤ Dealer ask prices
  - Compare prices of dealers at shows
- ➤ Condition
  - Note patina, wear and repairs
- ➤ Size
  - Unusual sizes are priced higher
- ➤ Rarity
- ➤ Maker
  - People are attracted to the well-known names.
- ➤ Provenance
  - Documented ownership increases value.
- ➤ Singles with mates
  - Singles are not valued as highly as a pair. If mate is built to match, the pair is not as valuable as the originals.
- ➤ Single or double mountings
  - A double-mounted pair of spurs is worth at least 20% more than single-mounted.
- ➤ Restoration
  - Quality restoration can enhance a piece.

Introduction

This Guide has been produced as a quick reference to 65 bit and spur makers who worked between 1870 and 1970 producing pieces in the Texas style. They were primarily in the states of Texas, Oklahoma, Kansas, New Mexico, and Arizona, as well as a few others.

For each maker, there is a portrait, a time line of when and where they worked, a photograph of their mark and examples of their craftmanship. Identifying characteristics of their style are described. There are also indications (for each maker who is no longer living) of

Collectibility (one* to five *****s)

Relative value (one$ to five $$$$$s)

Scarity one♦ to five ♦♦♦♦♦s)

These notations apply mainly to signed bits and spurs. If a piece is not marked by the maker, it is less valuable and less collectible unless he never signed his work at all. Collectibility is a relative masure and governed by personal preference. Often pieces are extremely desirable in the area in which their maker lived, but regarded with less interest in other places.

For a more complete biography of each maker, more photographs of their pieces in color, and a discussion of the history of the development of bit and spur styles, please see the more complete book on which this Guide is based: *Bit and Spur Maker in the Texas Tradition: a Historical Perspective*; available from Hawk Hill Press.

English silver curb bit of the late 1700s with saber cheek. Judy Gourley Collection.

French curb bit of 1700s. Ralph Emerson collection.

Spanish curb bit.

Mid 19ᵗʰ century saber cheek bits from New England. Ralph Emerson collection.

Chapter 1

Origins of Texas-style Bits and Spurs

Many believe Texas-style bits and spurs were made no earlier than the 1870s when J. C. Petmecky, a gunsmith from Austin, Texas, reputedly created a few patterns of spurs that almost immediately caught the fancy of local horsemen. Yet, nearly four hundred years of bit-and-spur making in the New World preceded Petmecky's first pair of spurs. The two most important contributors to the development of North American saddlery hardware were the Spanish and British, but the Dutch and the French also made bits and spurs which were used in North America.

In 1519, when Hernan Cortés. His horsemen and army passed through the gates of Mexico City, Spanish horse culture arrived in New Spain. Livestock as well as remnants of bits and spurs were left behind by several Spanish explorers in the sixteenth century; Cabeza de Vaca (1536), Coronado (1541), Espejos (1582), and Oñate (1598) were a prominent few among many. Through the 16th, 17th, and 18th centuries much of North America was a Spanish colony, and Spanish horse gear was widely used in Mexico and by the colonists in Florida, New Mexico, Texas, and California.

Meanwhile, the northeast was being settled by the Dutch and the English who brought their own styles of bits and spurs with them from Europe for use in the New World. Horses were coming into ports in New England as well as Jamestown, Virginia, and Charleston, South Carolina. For nearly two centuries, England supplied its American colonies with almost all of their saddlery hardware, although there is ample documentation that bits forged from simple patterns were made during the 18th century in all of the larger communities of the Northeast.

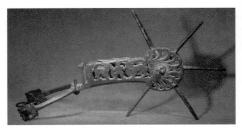
Conquistador spur of the 17th century.

19th Century Texas Settlement

At the dawn of the 19th century, Texas was a remote outpost of the vast colonial empire of Spain. Most of the horse gear was Spanish in style, made by Mexican blacksmiths. The Spanish officers and colonial land owners used fine bridles, bits, and spurs embellished with silver. The *vaqueros* herding cattle used Mexican ring bits made of iron or simple Mexican curb bits with slender cheeks. Their spurs were heavy and often ornate with large rowels.

Mexican curb bit.

Tex-Mex spurs. Kurt House collection.

In 1821 Mexico became independent of Spain, and Texas was henceforth a Mexican colony until it became an independent Republic in 1836. Meanwhile the *empressario*, Stephen Austin, was bringing large numbers of American settlers to his colony for free land. Other colonies were established, and the number of American settlers in Texas from the Northeast and the South increased rapidly. The bits and spurs they preferred were the English styles they brought with them, not the Mexican styles used by the enemy they fought many years for their independence. Throughout the 1830s and 1840s, relations between the Republic of Texas and Mexico were openly hostile, leading to the Mexican-American War in 1846-7.

19th century stubby bits made in the Northeast. Ralph Emerson and Judy Gourley collections.

In 1846 Texas became a state, and by then 55 to 60% of its population was Anglo-American. Most of the Anglos had close ties to the Southern states and the methods of farming and stock raising carried on in the new Texas colonies were essentially Southern. There were no industrial and manufacturing activities in Texas prior to 1850. Blacksmith-made curb bits were found throughout the South. They were of very simple practical construction with undecorated cheekpieces made from flat wrought iron stock. Low port mouthpieces were the rule, but made of narrower stock than present day mouth bars.

Texans supported the Confederacy in the Civil War, and after 1861, 2/3 of the white male population enlisted. During the war, Texas continued to export beef and cotton to support its people. During the Mexican-American War, as well as the Civil War, Southern soldiers became accustomed to using the military patterns of bits and spurs, which they continued to use when they returned to their Texas homes. An expanding cattle market fueled the economy of the growing state after 1880. The 1890s saw the emergence of a truly unique Texas style of bit and spur which is described in the following chapters.

Mexican spur and Confederate military spur.

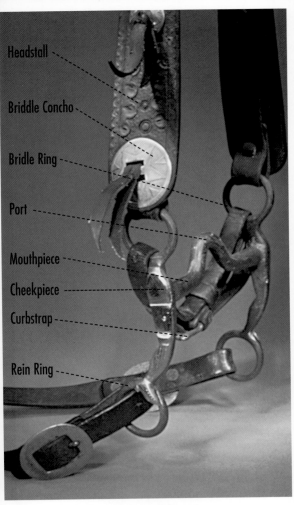

Headstall

Briddle Concho

Bridle Ring

Port

Mouthpiece

Cheekpiece

Curbstrap

Rein Ring

Component parts of a Texas curb bit. **Jess Hodge**, *maker.*

Simple curb bit manufactured by O. B. North of New Haven, CT in mid-1800s. Ralph Emerson collection.

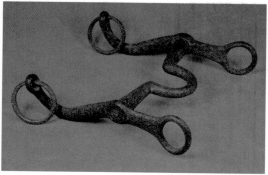

Gorham curb bit manufactured in the Northeast. Collection of Ralph Emerson.

Chapter 2

Texas Bits

The Texas or Southwestern-style curb bit has three basic components: a low port mouthpiece, short straight branches or cheeks with a minimal leverage factor, and a curb strap. Whether made on a production line by large manufacturing companies or forged in a one-man shop, the Texas-style bit was consistent in both size and shape, and in its simplicity of design and decoration. Whether the bit was manufactured in Oklahoma, Texas, Kansas, or Arizona, the style was identified as "Texas."

The unique Texas/Southwestern style evolved from the types of bits used in the Northeast and in the South, since the settlers who moved to Texas in the mid-19th century (1820-1870) brought their own bits. As former Confederate soldiers, these pioneers also tended to use the military styles popular during the Civil War.

Although Mexican horse accoutrements were common in Texas prior to 1821, they were never popular with later Texas-Americans settlers. In their practicality, Texans sought a simple, light-weight bit that could be made easily by local blacksmiths out of plain iron with no decoration and used on any horse. The Texas cowboy never used the Mexican ring bit style.

Comparison of Bit Styles

Texas/Southwest Tradition

Narrow cheekpieces
Often one-piece bits
Mostly low-port mouthpieces
Typically overlaid silver
Small area decorated
Stiff-jaw mouthpiece
Shorter shanks (average 6")
Ring bits not used
Rare use of cricket
Rare use of copper on mouthpiece
Occasional use of monel
No rein chains
No slobber bar
Plain leather reins
Used stainless steel
Recurring design motifs:
    gal-leg, mexican coins
Rare use of chased iron
Decorated with different shapes of
    silver mounting and minimal engraving
Combination of metals used in overlays

Comparison of Spur Styles

Texas/Southwest Tradition

One-piece spurs
Rare use of Mexican motifs
Stylish decoration
Usually overlaid silver
No heel chains
More stationary buttons
More stainless steel and monel
Straighter shanks
More utilitarian design
Rowels more blunt
Seldom used chased iron
No jinglebobs (*pajados*)
Heelbands often wide
Less use of chap guards
Recurring design motifs:
    gal leg, bottle opener, goose neck
Occasional use of nickel plating
Engraving patterns similar, while
    shapes of mountings varied.
Combinations of metals used
    in overlays: copper, silver, bronze.

Comparison of Bit Styles

California/Far West Tradition

Wider cheekpieces
No one-piece bits
Spade and half-breed preferred
Typically inlaid silver
Large area embellished
Loose-jaw mouthpiece
Longer shanks (average 7 1/2")
Ring bits common
Usually used cricket
Use of copper on mouthpiece
Monel used on occasion
Rein chains typical
Used slobber bar
Rawhide braided reins
Rare use of stainless steel
Recurring design motifs:
  snake, eagle, star, crescent moon
Some use of chased iron
Lavish engraving on overall silver mounting

Rarely used metals other than silver for inlays
  or overlays

Comparison of Spur Styles

California/Far West Tradition

Two-piece spurs
Mexican motifs popular
Elaborate ornamentation
Preferred inlaid silver
Always used heel chains
More swinging buttons
Stainless steel and monel rare
Preferred curved shank
More decorative design
Rowels sharper
Occasional chased patterns
Used jinglebobs
Most heelbands less than 1"
Most spurs have chap guards
Recurring design motifs:
  snake, eagle, star, crescent moon
Rarely nickel-plated
Greater variation in engraving
  patterns

A Mexican spur of the 18th century.

Texas-made Chihuahua spurs 1860s-1880s. Bruce Shakleford collection.

Mexican-made bottle-opener style spur from Kurt House collection.

Chapter 3

Texas Spurs

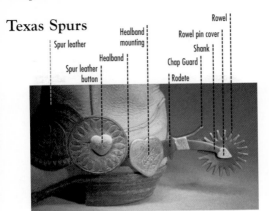

Spur leather

Spur leather
button

Healband

Healband
mounting

Rowel

Rowel pin cover

Shank

Chap Guard

Rodete

Rowel

Crockett three hearts spur from the Jay Lyndes collection.

In Texas and the Southwest, Mexican spurs were the most frequently used style during the early part of the 19th century. They were brought to the northern Mexican colony of Texas by *vaqueros* who herded the cattle, and by Spanish, followed by Mexican, soldiers who manned the colonial presidios until the 1830s. Meanwhile, American settlers from the Northeast and from southern states were moving to Texas in the 1820s and were bringing with them the English and French styles they had used before. The new settlers who developed ranches in eastern Texas in the Republic years used either Mexican or European-style spurs. There was no real indigenous style of spurs or bits in Texas until the end of the 19th century.

Spurs available to Texas cowboys from the 1840s to the 1870s were either produced by Mexican or Texas black-smiths or by Northeast manufacturers such as August Buermann and North & Judd. Mexican spurs, which had long been made in Amozoc, Mexico City, and Puebla de los Angeles, were used on large cattle ranch-es in the northern states of Mexico. These Mexican styles were copied, modified, and used primarily in West Texas well into the 20th century.

Many Texas cowboys were not satisfied with the heavy Mexican spurs. J. C. Petmecky of Austin, Texas, is given credit for being among the first to offer an alternatively stronger and lighter-weight one-piece spur made of tempered spring steel. Although Petmecky may have invented it around 1870, it was a New Jersey manufacturer, August Buermann, who made the improved spur widely available as the "O. K." style. From that time forward, after the Civil War, the typical Texas spur has been identified as a one-piece spur.

These two distinctly different spurs contrast the heavy, wide heel band, silver inlaid spurs made in Amozoc, Mexico, with J. C. Petmecky's light-weight, one-piece spur favored by many early Texas cowboys.

Design Motifs

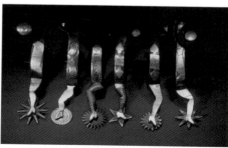

These six gal-leg spurs were each made by the following makers left to right: Kelly Bros., J. C. Petmecky, G. A. Bischoff, J. R. McChesney, C. P. Shipley, Jess Hodge.

Just as the pattern and shape of Texas spurs became identifiable, so also certain design motifs became popular in that part of America. The gal-leg pattern was perhaps the most characteristic one. It was used by the majority of Texas makers, especially those in mid and west Texas who preferred the wider heel bands. The gal-leg style varied from just the ankle and boot to a full leg of varying proportions. Sometimes a stylized leg was applied to the shank of a spur with silver mounting, and other times the iron itself was shaped into a realistic feminine form (including hips) by makers such as Petmecky, McChesney, and Bischoff. Tom Johnson, Sr. spurs almost always had a gal-leg pattern. Virtually all the makers of the gal-leg design, except Sam Allen, put a garter on the leg.

Another popular spur design was the bottle-opener which was most favored by south Texas makers such as Bianchi, Bego, Harvey, Traylor, and Thomas. It was later copied by all the large manufacturers including Huntsville prison makers. The style was earlier seen on Mexican spurs of the 18th century.

Bottle-opener spurs by Kelly Bros. Kurt House collection.

Animal heads were another design motif used on the shank of spurs. The gooseneck was especially popular with McChesney, Bass, Kelly, Crockett and Shipley as well as Buermann and North & Judd. The horse-head motif was perhaps used first in Texas by R. L. Causey, then by Kelly, Crockett, and Huff.

Horse-head spurs by K. B. & P. Ellis Ramsey collection.

Chapter 4

Marketing of Bits and Spurs

There were various ways for a cowboy to purchase bits and spurs. Word-of-mouth referral would direct him to the custom shop of someone like Bob Causey, Jess Hodge, or Tom Johnson. Alternatively, a buyer found bits and spurs at a local saddlery, which usually sold pieces made by Crockett, Kelly Bros., McChesney, and other Texas makers. The third and most common mechanism for purchase of cowboy gear was through mail order catalogs. All of the larger manufacturers published catalogs, as well as a few of the smaller makers such as Joe Bianchi, G. A. Bischoff, and J. O. Bass.

Most Texas bit-and-spur manufacturers, e.g., Kelly Bros. and Crockett, marked their pieces with their own name, despite distribution through a saddlery store. Perhaps the first Texas maker to mark his products was Austin gunsmith, J. C. Petmecky, although his maker-marked pieces are extremely rare. Apparently Petmecky marked his spurs with the same stamp he used to inscribe his guns.

The first Texas spur maker with significant output who marked his pieces consistently was G. A. Bischoff of Gainesville. The practice of inscribing bits and spurs became increasingly popular in the first decades of the 20th century as marketing tool. It served to distinguish a maker from his competitors. However, many artisans who were well-known in their own territory never marked their work: their style of forging, design, and engraving was a sufficient signature. The methods of marking metal usually involved the stamping of either individual letters or a group of letters (known as a gang stamp). These stamps were struck on the hot metal heel band or cheek piece before the parts were bent or welded together.

Johnnie Mullens spurs by McChesney. Abe Hayes Colletion.

The Beason Special spurs marked C. P. Shipley. Jay Lyndes collection.

Many saddleries published catalogs to advertise their own lines of saddles and other leather products. They frequently illustrated bits and spurs by other manufacturers in an attempt to offer a complete line of goods for the cowboy. Most catalogs generated more sales than the stores themselves, since the cowboys, who usually lived on isolated ranches, often shopped by mail. Bits and spurs were shown in most catalogs as line drawings and were identified by number.

In the 1920s, the manufacturers represented their spurs with names as well as numbers. The names ranged from towns, like the Cheyenne Special Miles City Special to cowboy celebrities names. The rodeo star spurs were extremely successful in the 1920s, and by 1931 virtually every model of spur carried a name. Whether named or numbered, pieces needed to be identified for ordering purposes.

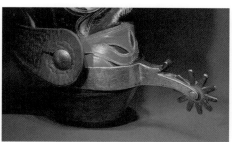

The Booger Red by O. Crockett. Jay Lyndes Collection.

Paddy Ryan spurs by Kelly Bros. Joe Flores collection.

List of Makers:

Allen, Sam
Bass, J.O.
Bayers, Adolph
Bego, Raymond
Bianchi, Joe
Blanchard, E.F.
Bischoff, G.A.
Boones: Clayton
            Bob
            Dee
            Pate
            Clyde
            Wallie
Bradney, Frank
Bryant, Louis
Browning & Murchinson
August Buermann
Causey, R.L.
Crockett, Oscar
Gilland, Jack
Grubb, L.G.
Hagelstein, Henry
Harvey, Frank
Hodge, Jess
Huff, O.R.
Johnson, Tom, Jr.
Kelly, P.M. & Kelly Bros.
K.B. & P.
K & C
Key, John Henry
Knowlton Bros.

Koenig, Karl
Kohler, E.J.
Kunshick, Julius
Kyle, Pettigrew & Moore
Longtine, Frank
McChesney, J.R.
Manriques, Lucio
Morales, Jesus
Nance, Joseph
North and Judd
Petmecky, Joseph Carl
Powder River
Prison Makers
Renalde
Ricardo
Schneider, Adolf
Shearer, Clay
Shipley, C.P.
Shirley, Earlon
Skelton, Red
Smith, Albert
Stephenson, Isaac
Strong, Harold
Studer, J.C.
Thomas, Bull
Traylor, Louie
Tucker, Fred
Weast, Willy
Wyatt, Charles H.
Zimmer, Henry C.
33 unknown makers listed
    from page 180 to 189.

SAMUEL THOMAS ALLEN
1876 - 1960

1876	Born near Ector, Fanin County, TX.
1880	Family moved to Gainesville, TX.
1880s	Cowboying.
1890s	Bought 500 acres of uncleared land on Red River.
1908	Married Helen Maude Graham. Working his own land and making bits and spurs in his blacksmith shop.
1918	Moved to Callisburg,TX. Bought 250 acres of land north of town.
1927	Moved back to his ranch on the Red River.
1960	Died at his home in Callisburg.

Allen made predominately gal-leg spurs with rounded legs and narrow ankles. He never put a garter on his gal legs. His work resembles McChesney pieces; He never marked his spurs.

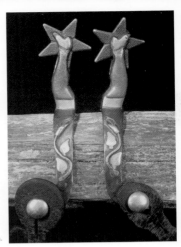

These Allen spurs have many of the characteristics of McChesney's trumpet vine motif. Frank Loftin collection.

Note the extremely naroow ankle and exaggerated calf on the gal-leg cheekpiece. In the background is a bronze cheekpiece of the Luristan period 2000 B.C. Ned Martin collection

J.O. BASS
1879 - 1950

★★★★★	$$$$$	◆◆◆
Collectibility	Value	Scarcity

1879	Born in Atlanta, Georgia.
1890	Moved to Young Co., TX.
1891	Moved to Quitaque in Panhandle of TX.
1897	J. O. opened his first blacksmith shop and made bits and spurs.
1905	Married Corrie, and moved to Tulia, TX, where he opened a new shop, making bits and spurs full time.
1910	Tom Mix and Texas Rangers began using his spurs.
1912	Issued catalogs.
1914	Won metalurgy award at Texas State Fair.
1924	Made his last pair of spurs. Farming full time.
1938	Moved to Plainview, Texas.
1950	Died of cancer in Marlin, Texas.

Bass preferred wide heel bands with card-suit motifs. One of his distinguishing characteristics was the heart-shaped spur leather buttons overlaid with half-copper, half silver. His swinging button hanger has a distinctive "hour glass" shape; His most common engraving pattern was the wheat stock. He marked most pieces. Bits have oval rein rings.

28

Bass marked his Quitaque bits and spurs on the outside of the piece as shown.

The above maker's marks illustrate how Bass marked his bits and spurs made in Tulia. He marked the bits sequentially beginning with 1 and continuing through approximately 800; spurs were numbered 1 to about 1846.

Bass patented this head stall ring "keeper" to separate the headstall from the curb strap.

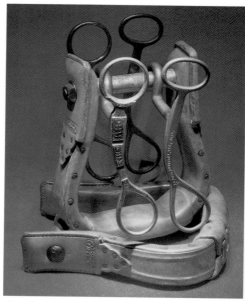

Classic bits of this important maker, the one on the right is typical of the Quitaque period and the bit on the left is a traditional Tulia-made piece with silver overlaid mountings.

Bass frequently used the card suit motif as a decorative element. This is his characteristic heart-shaped spur leather button half overlaid with copper. Kurt House collection.

Here is an example of Bass' largest spur each weighing one pound (8 1/2 inches with 4 1/2 inches rowel), mounted with silver Moorish motifs and smallest (4 1/2 inches with 1 inch rowel). Ellis Ramsey collection.

ADOLPH R. BAYERS
1912 - 1978

★★★★★	$$$$	◆◆
Collectibility	Value	Scarcity

1912	Born on a farm near Gilliland, Texas.
1920s	Worked on family farm and did metal work.
1930	Made first pair of spurs.
1942	Enlisted in U.S. Navy and worked as tool and die maker.
1946	Returned to Truscott, TX, to make bits and spurs.
1948	Married Fannie Lois Barker.
1955	Purchased McChesney tools.
1978	Died of cancer on the farm where he was born.

Bayers marked his spurs with his name and even number on the outside of the piece; each bit was marked with an odd number on the mouthpiece. He often overlaid the owner's name or initials on the off side of the spurs. He preferred wide heel bands, short shanks and small multi-pointed rowels. Swinging buttons used exclusively. His bits had oval rein rings.

Bayers marked his spurs with his name and even numbers on the outside of the piece; each bit was marked with an odd number on the mouthpiece. L. F. Blake collection.

These handsomely-crafted one-piece spurs illustrate the multi-pointed rowel often found on Bayers spurs. Jerry Cates Collection.

This unusually long cheek bit with oval shaped rein rings is characteristic of Bayer's bits.

RAYMOND BEGO
1900 - 1967

★★★	$$	◆◆◆◆◆
Collectibility	Value	Scarcity

1900	Born in Fanin, Texas, on a ranch.
1915	Training horses.
1920s	Married and had twin girls.
1938	Moved with family to Kilgore Community near Goliad.
1940s	Learned bit and spur making from Joe Bianchi. Ranching while making bits and spurs part time.
1967	Died of a heart attack.

Bego's spurs were predominately the bottle-opener style with flat heel bands of stainless steel. He frequently used Mexican coin mountings and buttons, and his pieces were not marked. He made a pinched port on bits.

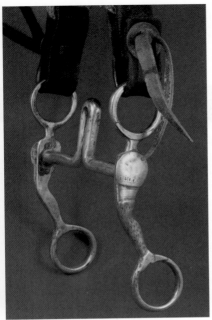

This gal-leg bit mounted with silver, copper, and brass reflects the influence of Joe Bianchi's pinched-port mouthpiece. There are few known examples of Bego's work. *Gentry Tomlinson collection.*

These spurs made for Gentry Tumlinson are decorated with Mexican coin rowel pin covers and spur leather buttons.

JOE BIANCHI
1871 - 1941

★ ★ ★ ★ ★	$$$$	◆ ◆ ◆
Collectibility	Value	Scarcity

1871	Born in Origgio, Italy.
1885	Family arrived in Victoria, Texas.
1901	Joined his brother Paul in Bianchi Bros. Blacksmith Shop.
1905	Married Mathilde Urban.
1909	Joe opened his own shop in Victoria, Texas, where he remained for 40 years. Made spurs for author Frank Dobie.
1919	Brother Paul died of influenza.
1920s	Produced a small catalog illustrating 4 bits and 4 spurs. Marked his spurs "Bianchi" on one spur and "Victoria TX" or "Hand Forged" on the other.
1938	Making bits and spurs out of stainless steel.
1949	Died in Victoria at age 78 after a long illness.

Bianchi made a characteristic bottle-opener style spur with rounded heel bands. He did not engrave his mountings. Most of his heel bands are less than 1/2 inch wide with stationary buttons and rowels with 8 to 12 points. He used Mexican domed coins as button and rowel pin covers. Bits have pinched-port mouthpieces and Mexican coins where the mouthpiece joins the cheek.

This is the most commonly seen of all the Bianchi marks **HAND FORGED**. It is thought to be the first mark that Joe Bianchi used.

Bianchi occasionally marked his spurs with this combination of marks inside the heelband. **J. Bianchi** inside on one spur and **VICTORIA TEX**, on the inside of the other side in the same sour.

This is an extremely rare maker's mark on Bianchi's "Close Mouth Piece."

Bianchi marked very few pieces **A.J. FIMBEL** which was the name of a saddlery in Victoria, Texas, that sold Bianchi bits and spurs.

This is one of the more popular styles of Bianchi spurs with his identifiable silver mountings without engraving. Note identifiable flat Mexican coin spur leather buttons. James A. McAllen collection

An unmarked bit by Joe Bianchi with a domed American coin (unlike his usual use of a domed Mexican coin).

This extremely rare bit represents a design popularized by Joe Bianchi with four Mexican coin conchos graduating in size. Shown as Bit No. 3 in Bianchi's catalog "C," this bit was available with either an "open" or "Close Mouth Piece" selling for $5.75 in 1925.

George A. Bischoff
1862 - 1944

★★★★★	$$$$$	◆◆◆◆◆
Collectibility	Value	Scarcity

1862	Born to German parents in Maryland.
1881	Completed apprenticeship in carriage factory in Maryland. Worked in several states and ended up in Dade City, Florida.
1890	Married Mollie Jane Tucker in Florida.
1894	Moved to Gainesville, Texas.
1895	Making bits and spurs, some of the time with McChesney.
1911	Published Catalog No. 1.
1915	Sold bit and spur business to C.P. Shipley and moved to Kansas City. Worked a few years at Shipley spur department.
1926	Moved to Oklahoma City.
1941	Worked for Douglas Aircraft in Tulsa, Oklahoma.
1944	Died in Tulsa, Oklahoma.

Bischoff is known for his very fine delicate engraving with unusual shapes. He often applied an elongated triangle with gold dot at the end and used double rows of wriggle engraving on the perimeter of mounting and a distinctive leaf motif engraving. Most of his spurs were double-mounted and made in one piece. He liked to apply different colored metals: yellow & red brass, copper, bronze, gold, & silver. He frequently used a gal-leg pattern with either a flat or round leg, some showing a hip. Made many more spurs than bits, marked most spurs, but not bits.

The G.A. BISCHOFF & CO. stamp which Bischoff used appears in three different sizes. The earliest known Bischoff mark used letters 1/16 inch in height. Only on the pieces that are marked with this smallest stamp did Bischoff include the mark HAND FORGED. Both of these marks appear inside the heelband on each spur of the pair. The next being 1/8 inch, and the last pieces were marked a 1/4 inch stamp. He used a gang stamp to mark his spurs, and only one bit is known that is marked **G.A. BISCHOFF & CO.**

Double mounted gal-legs showing the classic Bischoff hip. The engraved silver overlaid elongated triangle ending with a gold dot illustrates an identifiable pattern often seen on Bischiff's pieces.

Elegant in its simplicity.

Details characteristic of Bischoff engraving, and his identifiable double wriggle border engraving and leaf motif which he frequently used. Ellis Ramsey collection.

It is the opinion of most collectors that Bischoff's gal-leg spurs and rowel patterns best exemplify these elegant shapes that were used by many Texas bit-and-spur makers. Bischoff offered twelve different rowel choices on his one-piece spurs, more than any other Texas maker. Bischoff identified these spurs are style "F", "S", "H", "W", "N", "M", "T", "H". Ellis Ramsey collection.

EDWARD FRED BLANCHARD
1894 - 1982

★★★	$$	◆◆◆
Collectibility	Value	Scarcity

1894	Born in Magdalena, New Mexico.
1914	Enlisted in W.W. I.
1920s	Managing family ranch and making some spurs.
1930s-'40s	Living with sister in Monticello, NM, and working summers in Datil, NM. Making spurs and bits.
1948-9	Cowboyed in San Antonio, New Mexico.
1952	Cowboyed in Seligman County, Arizona.
1955	Bought a ranch and moved near Yucca, Arizona.
1970	Mailed out a folder showing six spurs he would make. Moved into the town of Yucca, Az.
1982	Died in Kingman, Arizona.

Blanchard spurs were characterized by very wide heel bands with swinging buttons and multi-pointed, small diameter rowels. Early pieces were made of iron, and his later production was stainless steel. There are no known bits made by Blanchard. He marked most of his pieces.

Earliest Blanchard marks. **E.F. BLANCHARD MONTICELLO N.M.**

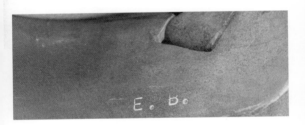

Marked spurs with initials **E. B.** *inside one spur, and* **DATIL N.M.** *inside the other.*

When in San Antonio, N.M. he marked his spurs with his name and location.

The next mark used was a stamp with **E.F. BLANCHARD SELIGMAN ARIZ.** *inside one spur.*

This maker's mark is the last one that he used when his shop was located in Yucca, Ariz.

These one-piece iron spurs marked E.B., DATIL, N.M. exemplify an early period production. This style No. 6 with 1 1/2 inch heelbands without silver mounting is characteristic of Blanchard spurs. Cowboys favored Blanchard's spurs as they fit the boot like no other. Bruce Bartlett collection.

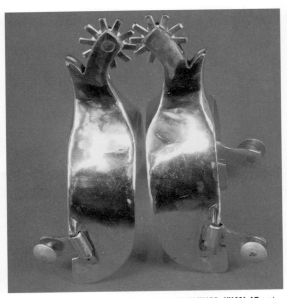

These stainless steel two-piece spurs marked **E.F. BLANCHARD. YUCCA AZ** *with slanted button hangers are shown as style No. 4 in Blanchard's brochure. This is the only style of spur that he made with a chap guard.* Sonny Parsons collection.

JERRY CLAYTON BOONE
1853 - 1947

★★★	$$$	◆◆◆◆◆
Collectibility	Value	Scarcity

1853	Born in North Carolina.
1865	Left home alone and traveled to Greenvine, Texas. He lived and worked there with his Uncle Tom, a blacksmith.
1870s	Married Frances Abigail Campbell and worked on her father's farm.
1889	Packed wife, three children and household goods in a wagon and moved to Round Timber, Texas.
1900	Moved to Trent, Texas.
1901	To Midland, Texas.
1902	To Monument, New Mexico.
1906	Back to Trent, Texas. Bob and Pate start their Wild West Show.
1912	Settled in Decatur, Texas, and set up a blacksmith shop. Clayton made more spurs there than anywhere else.
1918	Moved to Pittsburg, Oklahoma. Made bits and spurs with son, Dee, and did general blacksmithing.
1947	Died in Hobbs, New Mexico

THE BOONES

JERRY CLAYTON BOONE (FATHER)
1853 - 1947

BOB BOONE (SON)
1883 - 1974

THOMAS PAYSON "PATE" BOONE (SON)
1887 - 1980

DEE BOONE (SON)
1898 - 1976

CLYDE BOONE (SON)
1900 - 1960

WALLIE BOONE (NEPHEW)
1882 - 1958

CHARLES ROBERT "BOB" BOONE
1883 - 1974

★★★★★	$$$$$	◆◆◆◆◆
Collectibility	Value	Scarcity

1883 Born in Greenvine, Texas.

1889 Moved with family to Round Timber, Texas. There he learned from his father to make bits and spurs, and even as a boy he made them to sell.

1898 Family moved to Clyde, where Bob made his first pair of gal-leg spurs.

1900 Worked full time in Trent, Texas, with his father as a blacksmith and bit and spur maker. He put out a catalog and sold bits and spurs by mail.

1901 Family moved to Midland and opened a shop where Clayton was blacksmith, and Bob worked as full-time bit and spur maker.

1906 Returned to Trent after living awhile in Monument, New Mexico. Bob and brother Pate started Wild West Show which traveled all over Texas and neighboring states.

1912 Married Mary Jane Green. They lived in a wagon, then a railroad car, and worked for the Wild West Show.

1918 Left the Wild West Show and settled with wife and child in Gordon, Kansas, where they had three more children. Bob worked dressing tools for the oil fields. Later he joined his family in Pittsburg, Oklahoma, and worked in coal mine tool shop.

1931 Homesteaded 640 acres in Ramon, New Mexico, where he did ranching and blacksmithing. His two sons worked on ranch.

Charles Robert "Bob" Boone
1883 - 1974

(Con't)

1938	Moved to Albuquerque where he made custom-ordered bits and spurs.
1942	Moved to Burbank, California, and worked in an aircraft plant. Later made fancy engraved and inlaid bits and spurs to order.
1974	Died in San Diego, California.

One of the finest Texas makers, Bob did innovative pierced iron work with chased motifs. He engraved and inlaid his multi-pointed spur rowels. He made more spurs than bits and his spurs had more creative designs than did his bits. Not many of his pieces were marked, but they command the highest prices.

Early Bob Boone marks while in Midland, Texas. 1901-05. Although not shown there is a known example of a bit marked Trent, Texas.

Later period mark of Boone.

This extremely rare pair of Boone spurs exemplifies the creativity of one of the finest Texas bit and spur makers. Bob Boone's innovative techniques included the use of pierced shapes and silver dots as a decorative element.
Rich Bullard collection.

Embellished with inlaid Mercury dimes, these unmarked double mounted spurs are attributed to Bob Boone. The off side is exquisitely detailed engraving on the iron heel-band with flower motifs and scalloped edges.

Suprisingly Bob Boone's bits are relativity simple in comparison to his handsomely crafted spurs. This bit is marked **Bob Boone, Midland, TEX**.

Few Texas makers employed the technique of engraving the iron. Bob Boone ornamented this spur with a heart and vine motif on the off-side, and engraved silver on the other side as shown in the accompanying detail.

THOMAS PAYSON "PATE" BOONE
1887 - 1980

★★★	$$	♦♦♦♦
Collectibility	Value	Scarcity

1887	Born in Greenvine, Texas.
1890s	Family moved around Texas and all the boys helped their Dad in his blacksmith work.
1905	Made his first pair of spurs, and Bob put silver on them for him and engraved his intials. At age 17 Pate and brother Bob started their Wild West Show. Pate married.
1922	Wild West Show closed, Pate made no bits or spurs during the show years. Joined his Father and brothers in Pittsburg, Oklahoma, and made some bits and spurs with brothers.
1930	Pate had a blacksmith business in Kilgore, Texas.
1933	Living in Houston.
1936	Living in Hobbs, New Mexico, for 18 years.
1954	Moved to Christoval, Texas, for his wife's health. Had an antique store and made wagons and spurs.
1980	Died in Christoval.

Pate made giant spurs as novelty items. His pieces are crude and seem relatively unfinished. The gal-leg motif is common. Some marks have backward N. or PATE BOONE.

These two maker's marks are attributed to Pate Boone according to Boone expert and collector Larry Boyd. He also used the mark **PATE BOONE**.

WALLIE BOONE
1880 - 1958

★★★	$$$	◆◆◆
Collectibility	Value	Scarcity

1880	Son of Duff Boone, blacksmith, cousin of Clayton Boone.
1900	Learned bit and spur making from cousin Bob in Trent, Texas.
1924	Established Boone's Bits and Spurs in Lubbock, Texas.
1930s	Wallie working as blacksmith in village of Whiteflat, Texas.
1936	W.R. Boone Co, Blacksmiths. Company in San Angelo, Texas, made braces for Model T fenders, and then made bits and spurs.
1940	Clyde worked with him in San Angelo.
1945	Went to prison for killing a man.
1949	Boone Bits and Spurs bought out by Jack Fuqua.
1950s	Moved to Andrews, Texas, to live with his sister.
1958	Died in a rest home in Rosco, Texas.

Wallie made roper and bronc-style spurs, predominately with short shanks. He originated nickel-plated finishes, used a wriggling technique for textured backgrounds, embossed decorative motifs, and marked pieces with thick individual letter stamps. Stamford Rodeo programs confirm that his spurs, with mounted plaques reading "Texas Centennial 1936" and "Stamford Cowboy Reunion 1931" were given as prizes at the rodeo.

Wallie Boone's maker's mark on the outside of the heelband, under the button.

Wallie stamped most of his spurs **BOONE** on the inside of the heelband as shown. Frequently Boone reversed the **N** when marking a piece (perhaps just a mistake). Wallie did not mark all of his work.

Wallie Boone frequently used the motif shown on this marked **BOONE** low-port Texas-style bit.

Typical Wallie Boone spurs shown in his catalog as No.27 with 5/8 inch heelbands and 1 1/2 inch 8 point rowel. The No.27 is the most common mounted pattern that Wallie made. Bruce Barlett collection.

Wallie Boone identified this spur as No.3 "THE KENT, TEXAS". Boone's individual style is easily distinguished by the short shank and wriggling of his backgrounds on his spurs. Fleisher collection.

CLYDE CAMPBELL BOONE
1900 - 1960

★★★	$$	◆◆◆◆◆
Collectibility	Value	Scarcity

1900	Born in Trent, Texas, the fourth and youngest son of Clayton. Grew up in Trent working in the blacksmith shop with his father and brothers and helped with Wild West Show. Roping.
1919	Serious case of Typhoid Fever weakened his heart.
1920s	Painted billboards and barn signs as well as gold leaf decor.
1927	Married Margaret C. Mackey. Raised 2 sons and a daughter.
1940s	Painted signs on outfield fences of baseball parks. Worked for Wallie in San Angelo in early '40s, and with brother Pate in Hobbs, NM in the late 1940s.
1955	Living in Christoval working with Pate in blacksmith shop. Making spurs and carving wooden oxen yokes.
1960	Died in Christoval of heart problems.

DANIEL "DEE" BOONE
1898 - 1976

★★ Collectibility	$$ Value	◆◆ Scarcity

1898	Born in Round Timber, Texas, and when just weeks old the family moved to Clyde.
1904	Dee made his first pair of spurs in Trent, Texas.
1912	Family living in Decatur.
1915	Dee left home to join his brothers' Wild West Show.
1918	Left Wild West Show and worked in a shop across from his father's. Moved to Pittsburg, Oklahoma, and had a shop in his house where he made bits and spurs to order; also broke horses. All pieces were overlaid. He never made inlays.
1927	Moved to Henryetta, Oklahoma with wife, Atta Rogers (niece of Will Rogers). They had one daughter. He had a blacksmith shop in Henryetta for the next 45 years where he made and repaired bits and spurs and knives. Also a gunsmith. (In trouble with government over making guns without a license.) General blacksmith and horseshoer.
1971	Closed blacksmith shop in town and continued same work at home.
1976	Died of a heart attack in Henryetta, Oklahoma.

Dee's pieces were not as refined as other Boone's spurs. He made some very large proportion bits and spurs. He frequently added no mountings, but occasionally used copper overlays. He marked his work with individual letter stamps.

60

Dee Boone used individual letters to mark his work. Note the slight angle of the E, this appears to be a characteristic of Dee Boone marks. Dee never chose to have a gang stamp made.

This unusually proportioned full-bodied lady curb bit is marked D. BOONE. Dee is known for his oversized pieces of which this is a classic example.

Marked Dee Boone, these unusual shaped gal-leg spurs with Cheyenne split heelband are a fine example of Dee's craftsmanship. Note the silver-overlaid shoes which are double-mounted on these 7 1/4 inch long spurs. These are from the H.C. Lewis collection which sold at the Butterfield & Butterfield auction in San Francisco in 1989.
Ellis Ramsey collection.

FRANK L. BRADNEY
1913 - 1999

★★★★	$$$	◆◆◆
Collectibility	Value	Scarcity

1913	Born near Higgins, Texas. Learned black-smithing from his father.
1930s	Working with Isaac Stephenson to make bits and spurs. Married and after a few years divorced. Had one son, Jim.
1940s	Married Nora Lee and had one daughter. Moved to Amarillo.
1948	Moved to Grand Canyon to work with mules. Married Billie there.
1960s	Moved to Colorado. Went to Canyon City Prison for 12-15 years.
1970s	Moved to Camp Verde, Arizona, making bits and spurs.
1988	Moved to Hollis, Texas.
1999	Died in a nursing home in Hollis.

Frank's spurs had wide heel bands, short shanks, small diameter rowels, and swinging buttons. His engraving style was very simple, and he frequently had brass initials overlaid on silver.

Bradney marked his spurs with the stamp **BY. F.B.**

Bradney made these spurs for himself with his initials in brass overlay.
Wayne Paul collection.

Bradney used a consistent identifiable pattern of wide heelbands
and short shanks. *Charles Forbe Collection.*

NOBLE CICERO BROWNING AND WALTER P. MURCHISON

★★★★★	♦♦♦♦♦
Collectibility	$$$$ Value	Scarcity

1877	N. C. Browning born in Texas.
1898	N. C. Browning married Vera Harwood.
1902	N. C. Browning had son, Lewis, born in Gainesville, TX.
1907	Browning working with McChesney.
1912	Browning with Bischoff.
1915	Browning went to Tulia with Bass.
1903	Murchison born.
1920s	Murchison in Canyon, TX.
1980	Murchison died and buried at Spur, Dickens County. Browning and Murchison open a shop in Plainview, TX.

Very rare mark of **B & M** *representing the partnership of Browning & Muchison*

They made thick heavy spurs with beveled edges on shanks and used copper mountings. Their refined delicate bits were intricately engraved. They marked pieces in several ways.

This stamp reads **MAKER W.P. MURCHISON CANYON TEX**. *This maker's mark is the only Canyon one known to exist.*

Browning & Murchison marked these one-piece spurs with their initials **B.&M.** *with engraved silver and copper mountings. Note the identifiable beveled edges on the shanks.* Kurt House Collection.

This quintessential bit of the Texas twenties features a full flapper figure exquisitely engraved. This bit is marked **B. & M.** *on the edge of the cheek.* Ned Martin collection.

LOUIS BRYANT
1919 - 2000

★★★	$$$	◆◆◆
Collectibility	Value	Scarcity

1919	Born in Hollis, Oklahoma.
1932	Blacksmith father unable to work, so Louis began working in blacksmith shop full time.
1940	Served in World War II for one year. Returned to work welding storage tanks until injured.
1940s	Went to college to become a medical lab technician.
1970	Retired from years working as a lab technician and began making jewelry.
1979	Returned to Tecumseh, Oklahoma, with wife, Willie Dee, and resumed making bits and spurs.
1999	Had a stroke and stopped making bits and spurs.
2000	Died in a nursing home.

Bryant made a one-piece spur and bit. His styles were influenced by Bischoff.

Bryant marks his pieces with a gang stamp on the outside of the spur and inside of the bit cheekpiece.

These one-piece spurs reflect the influence of G.A. Bischoff.

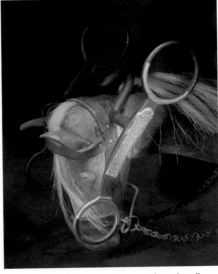

Bryant is one of the few contemporary makers who still makes a one-piece bit. Ned Martin collection.

BUERMANN MANUFACTURING CO.
1866 - 1926

AUGUST BUERMANN
1842 - 1928

★★★	$$$	◆
Collectibility	Value	Scarcity

1863	August Buermann arrived in U.S. and worked for Alexander Barclay & Co. in Newark, NJ.
1864	He was paid to take someone's place as a soldier in the Union Army. He served for one year.
1866	Buermann bought Barclay & Co.
1871	Brief partnership with Hartman.
1902	Plant expanded to a four-storey brick building in Newark.
1926	North and Judd acquired Buermann Company.

Mass production of regional styles from Texas, California, Mexico. This company had the ability to copy individual makers' products: Bianchi, McChesney, Kelly, Crockett, etc. They used metal alloys, and were the earliest to use plating. Their pieces were embellished with chasing, engraving, overlay, and inlay techniques. Each piece was marked.

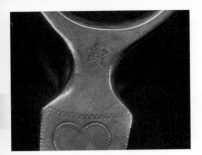

The most common Buermann mark was a star with the initials **AB** inside, however, an earlier mark had the **AB** outside with a letter on each side of the star.

Also used as a maker's mark was the stamp **HAND FORGED STEEL**

Two-button Eureka spur which was available through Sears, Roebuck and Company for 50 cents a pair in their 1897 catalog.

This Buermann bit with it's pinch port is reminiscent of Joe Bianchi's classic bit with similar mouthpiece. Ralph Emerson collection.

*Here is an example of a curb bit which is about as Texas as you can get. Marked with Buermann's Star with inside **AB**. This bit illustrates the use of the frequently seen card suit motif.*

Marked with Buermann's **FORGED STEEL** stamp, these spurs are shown in his catalog No. 35 as spur No. 1145. The same spur is also shown in the catalog of the following makers as a pattern which they manufactured, Crockett, Kelly, C.P. Shipley, McChesney, and Wallie Boone. The style of this spur is commonly known as the Johnnie Mullens.
George Brown collection.

This is Buermann's most noted spur "Genuine Patent O.K. Spurs" one-piece. There are six different styles offered in his catalog. Buermann acquired the design from J.C. Petmecky who originated this pattern; however it was Buermann who popularized this spur.
Charles Forbes collection.

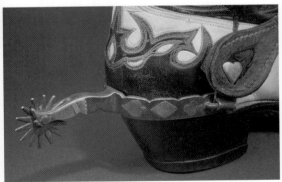

Buermann's rendition of the traditional Texas gal-leg with card suit mountings.
Kurt House collection.

ROBERT LINCOLN CAUSEY
1868 - 1937

★★★★★	$$$$$	◆◆◆◆◆
Collectibility	Value	Scarcity

1868	Born in Kansas City, KS, one of 10 children of blacksmith father.
1880	Boarded a train alone to go to the Indian Territory (Oklahoma). Worked in blacksmith shop for room and board.
1884	Joined brother George on a ranch in Lovington, New Mexico.
1888	Moved to Odessa, Texas, and opened a blacksmith shop.
1890s	Blacksmithing in Eddy, New Mexico.
1903	Married Martha Agnes Bogle.
1906	Moved to Artesia, New Mexico with wife and daughter. Causey and Osborn had blacksmith business together.
1910	Making bits and spurs in Pendleton, OR, and Rupert, ID, before returning to Carlsbad, NM.
1924	Moved to Safford, AZ, as a full time bit and spur maker.
1937	Died at home in Safford, AZ.

Causey frequently used the gal-leg design, and used copper, brass, and silver for mountings. He was one of few Texas-style makers to inlay his work. His mountings have minimal engraving, and he frequently used chased iron designs and multi-pointed decorative rowels. He only occasionally marked his work.

Not all of Causey's pieces are marked, those that are have the early mark of his initials **RLC** incised on the inside of the spur heelband. His later period pieces are stamped **RLC** for Robert Lincoln Causey. Grady Stowe collection.

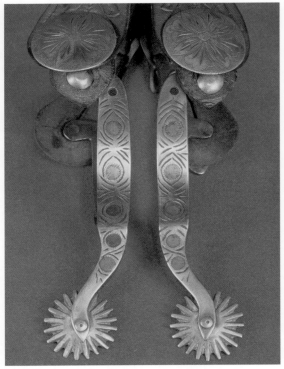

Marked **RLC.**, this is an example of a pair of spurs that have chased iron pattern, and silver inlay. Causey was one of the few Texas makers proficient in both skills. Grady Stowe collection.

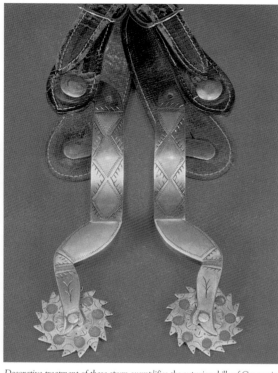

Decorative treatment of these spurs exemplifies the superior skills of Causey in combining silver inlay, and chased iron (the term chasing implies no metal was removed.) These gal-leg spurs are marked with his initials **RLC**. *Note the embellished saw-tooth rowels with silver inlaid circles. Grady Stowe collection.*

This spur, with the extremely rare mark CAUSEY & OSBORN, is from the period when Osborn and Causey were partners in 1906. Otis Hibler collection.

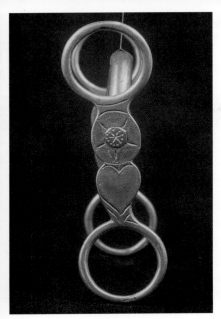

*There are few known examples of Causey bits; this one is stamped with his initials **R L C** on the port.*
Dick Powell collection.

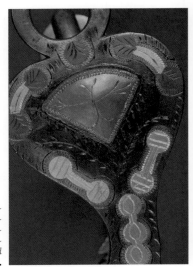

*Distinctively characteristic of Causey. This innovative bit design combining inlaid copper and silver, chased iron, and marked on the port **R L C**.*

OSCAR CROCKETT
1887 - 1949

★★★★★	$$$$$	◆◆◆◆◆
Collectibility	Value	Scarcity

1887	Born in Pecos City, TX.
1900s	Watched older brother, Arthur, make bits and spurs.
1910	In Kansas City working in blacksmith shop; making bits and spurs at night.
1914	Partnered with George Gliem; C&G Bits and Spurs after hours.
1915	Split with Gliem; retained ownership of C&G line.
1916	Sold C&G line to Shipley; opened a shop in Pawhuska, OK.
1917	Closed Pawhuska shop; moved to Bremerton, WA, WW I shipyards.
1919	Oscar and Arthur making bits and spurs for Shipley in Kansas City.
1920	Bought Shipley bit and spur dept.; began Crockett Bit and Spur Co.
1927	Oscar bought out his uncle, W.B. (Brice) Crockett.
1932	Married Hazel Miller, moved home and shop to farm at Lenexa, KS.
1943	Moved factory and ten workers to Boulder, CO in wartime.
1948	Left for Lenexa to ready the farm for sale.
1949	Died of a heart attack in Boulder; buried in Kansas City.

Oscar's pieces were characterized by his raised rowel pin cover and the spur button engraved with a quadrant pattern.

CROCKETT BIT AND SPUR COMPANY
1920-1985

By Bill Adamson

★ Collectibility	$ Value	◆ Scarcity

1920	Oscar Crockett bought the bit and spur department of Shipley Saddlery and Mercantile in Kansas City, Missouri.
1927	Produced 5000 pairs of spurs and 5000 bits.
1932	Moved factory to Lenexa, KS.
1943	Moved the company to Boulder, Colorado.
1951	Company sold to James Renalde.
1965	Added Kelly line to become Crockett-Renalde and Kelly.
1971	Death of James Renalde.
1973	Reorganization; the bank installed Larry Lythgoe manager.
1977	Receivership; Hank Kugeler and Bob Harrison were the new owners/managers.
1980	Horst family new owners. Crockett and Kelly, Inc. in Broomfield, CO.
1984	Crockett and Kelly, Inc. ceased production.
1985	Auctioned bit and spur inventory.

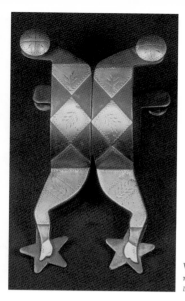

Wide heelband, inside marked **CROCKETT & GLIEM.**
Lawson and Nancy Walden collection.

"THE MIDDLE WEST" No.210 as shown in Crockett catalog 12. An extremely rare three heart pattern outside marked **CROCKETT** *spurs.*
Jay Lyndes collection.

Illustrated as spur No.151 Crockett Catalog 14 with Cheyenne split heelband marked **O. CROCKETT**. *Shown is the characteristic Crockett spur button engraved with the four quadrant pattern.* Jay Lyndes collection.

These spurs are mounted with copper and silver as a decorative treatment. Charles Forbes collection.

Silver overlaid gal-leg pattern outside marked **CROCKETT**.
Bill Adamson collection.

This innovative design on a curb bit of a silver overlaid arrow cheekpiece is handsomely crafted.

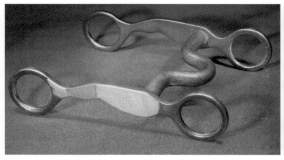

Two-piece gal-leg engraved copper and silver overlaid mounted curb bit.
Bill Adamson collection.

Mark	Size	Location	Time	Comments
Early Years				
CROCKETT & GLEM KAN CITY MO		1,1A	1914-16	
CROCKETT	11/16"**	1,	1915-16 (K.C), 1916-17 (PAWHUSKA)	0 irregularly used/positioned, sometimes with KAN CITY MO
0. CROCKETT	1"*	1,1A	1917-1924	In K.C., maybe Pawhuska, OK
CROCKETT	1-1/4"*	1,1A	1925-35	Big inside mark
Middle Years				
CROCKETT	1/16"**	2	1935-38	Earliest outside mark
CROCKETT	3/22"***	2	1938-43	2nd outside mark
CROCKETT	1/16"- 3/22"***	3	1943-46	3rd outside mark
After Oscar				
CROCKETT		4,5	1946-55	Transition, three sizes of marks
(C)		2,6,7	1953-77	Most common on swinger
RC/K		2	1976-79	Crockett, Kelly, Renalde
CROCKETT		2	1980-84	Small mark similar to early outside mark
CROCKETT USA		2	1984-85	Used on blanks at 1985 liquidation auction

* Length dimension applies to CROCKETT portion of mark

** Height dimension of letters.

Notes: The above refers to the major populations of production. Numerous exceptions exist.
There is evidence that some of the long-time Crockett retailers insisted on the Crockett mark well
into the 1960s.

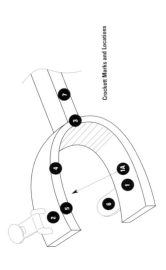

Crockett Marks and Locations

John Wiley "Jack" Gilland
1891 - 1969

★★	$$	◆◆◆◆◆
Collectibility	Value	Scarcity

1891	Born in Plano, Collin County, Texas.
1918	Left ranch in Foard County to work on pipeline.
1921	Returned to Good Creek Community, Foard County.
1922	Began working on the Y Ranch.
1947	Married Audy.
1960	Retired and returned to Good Creek near Crowell, Texas.
1969	Died and was buried in Crowell.

Gilland sometimes mounted his pieces with silver hearts, but often added no mounting at all. Most of his spurs have comparatively short, straight shanks, wide heel bands and swinging buttons on a staple.

Shop-forged spurs spray-painted gold with silver mountings and Indian head nickel buttons. Betty Gilland collection.

LEONARD G. GRUBB
1900 - 1989

★★	$$$	◆◆◆◆
Collectibility	Value	Scarcity

1900	Born in Thomaston, Georgia. Moved to Texas at the age of six months.
1907	Moved to Swisher County near Kress, Texas.
1916	Made first spurs after watching J. O. Bass.
1934	Married Vera Stewart of Swisher County. Moved to farm south of Tulia.
1936	Birth of only son, Leonard Norwood Grubb.
1960	Retired from farming and resumed making bits and spurs.

Grubb used brass strips inlaid on a diagonal pattern. He preferred heart-shaped buttons. His pieces are marked with his name and the date made. His bits show the influence of J. O. Bass.

Grubb marked his work with his name and date using individual letter stamps.

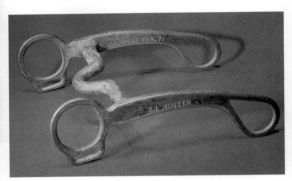

This two-piece iron bit made by Grubb shows J.O. Bass' influence.
Mack White collection.

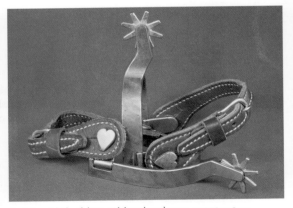

Steel spurs inlaid with brass with brass heart buttons. Mack White collection.

CHRIS HAGELSTEIN
1844 - 1915

★★★★
Collectibility

$$$
Value

◆◆◆◆◆
Scarcity

1844	Born in Oering, Prussia, now Denmark.
1871	Immigrated to the U.S.A.
1883	Came to Concho County, Texas; blacksmithed for U.S. soldiers from Fort Concho at San Angelo, TX.
1884	Married Emma Winkle and settled in new town of Paint Rock, TX where they remained to raise five children. Blacksmithing and made bits and spurs as a sideline.
1905	Appointed postmaster and served until end of 1914.
1915	Died in Paint Rock.

Hagelstein bits have a 1" metal concho stamped C.HAGELSTEIN Paint Rock Tex. His spurs have wide heel bands and no mountings. His spurs are not marked.

Few makers marked their bits as distinctly as this maker as shown **C. HAGELSTEIN PAINT ROCK. TEX.** *with his name and location on the conchos. There is one other known example of a bit marked with his name and San Angelo, Tex.*

Unmarked iron spurs with no decoration. These spurs were purchased from Hagelstein and have remained in the Paint Rock area over sixty years. Note unusual 2 3/4 inch four-pointed rowel. A horse might not take kindly to these.
Kurt House collection.

Hagelstein bits are easily identified by the large conchos marked **C. HAGELSTEIN PAINT ROCK TEX.**

FRANK M. HARVEY
1876 - 1944

★★★	$$	◆◆◆◆◆
Collectibility	Value	Scarcity

1876	Born in Wallisville, TX.
1890s	Working in wheelright shop with father.
1900	Making bits and spurs on his own. Married Atta Pearl Ewell and lived in Cedar Bayou.
1907	Moved to Crosby, Texas; built a house and blacksmith shop.
1913	With others, founded Crosby State Bank.
1940s	Making knives for friends in World War II; He had a stroke.
1944	Died and was buried in Crosby.

This seldom seen maker's mark is stamped on the bottom edge of the heelband. Occasionally Harvey included his initial F with his mark.

Harvey made his pieces out of stainless steel. He preferred the bottle-opener style of spurs and used a peculiar spade-tipped rowel and Mexican silver peso buttons. Most of his pieces are marked.

Stainless steel bottle-opener spurs with wriggle engraving vine pattern and large Mexican silver peso buttons. One can immediately see Joe Bianchi's influence.
Cynthia Williams collection.

JESS HODGE
1870 - 1953

★★★★★	$$$$	◆◆◆◆
Collectibility	Value	Scarcity

1870	Born in Alabama.
1912	Worked for the XIT Ranch in Panhandle of Texas.
1915	Opened shop in Fort McKavett, Texas.
1953	Died in Brady Nursing Home.

Hodge made spurs with beveled edges on the shanks, octagonal buttons, oblong-shaped silver rowel-pin covers, and silver overlaid "T" mountings at the junction of the shank with the heel band. He used a slender extended gal-leg design, and liked a long horn steer motif as mounting. There was a wide variation in the quality of his engraving and he frequently applied copper, brass and silver mountings. He used galvanized windmill fan blades for button hangers, and employed a hacksaw to cut slots for rowels. His bits have oval rein rings. He did not mark his pieces.

Note elongated rowel-pin cover

These gal-leg spurs made by Hodge of an identifiable pattern commonly called "frog leg style." Another distinguishing feature is the octagon shape spur button, the right button is missing and the rowel is atypical. *Ernie Davis collection.*

Characteristic octagon-shaped spur buttons. Hodge's engraving is identifiable by its simple style "walking the flat" accomplished by use of a wriggling technique. *Wayne Mitchell collection.*

Detail of steer-head silver mounting at heelband and shank junction.
Ernie Davis collection.

Very unusual elongated gal-leg curb bit with minimal engraving on silver and copper mountings. Hodge's later pieces show less refinement of engraving compared to his earlier work.

OLIVER REDUS HUFF
1902 - 1983

★★★		$$		◆◆◆◆
Collectibility		Value		Scarcity

1902	Born near Boyd in Wise County, TX.
1923	Moved to Fort Worth, worked for Armour & Co.
1930s	Made spurs in his garage most of his life.
1950s	Bought 100 longhorn steer heads, mounted and sold them.
1963	Retired; collected guns and spurs.
1968	Daughter moved home to Ft. Worth to care for sick mother.
1983	He died at home.

Huff marked his spurs either "O. R. HUFF" or with his grandfathers brand "D+"

Many of the spurs Huff made use the innovative design of a horse-head as a decorative motif. Here the use of brass overlay to define the bridle, the rattlesnake heelbands, and maker's mark using the family brand is masterfully handled. *Cliff Logan collecion.*

These elegant double-mounted silver-overlaid spurs with colored stones feature Huff's distinctive horsehead design. This is the last pair of spurs made by O.R. Huff. *National Cowboy and Western Heritage Center.*

THOMAS A. JOHNSON
1875 - 1915

★★★★ $$$$ ◆◆◆◆
Collectibility   Value   Scarcity

1875	Born the son of a blacksmith in Arkansas.
1890	Blacksmith shop with his father in Coleman, Texas: Johnson and Son, Blacksmiths.
1900	Had his own shop in Coleman, Texas. Married to Irma.
1905	Making bits and spurs in Albany, Texas.
1910	Worked with McChesney in Paul's Valley, OK.
1911	Moved to Dalhart, TX, to work with P.M. Kelly.
1911	Married Kelly's sister, Lena May.
1912	Started his own business of bit and spur making in Dalhart.
1915	Died of kidney failure in Dalhart, Texas.

Tom Johnson never marked his pieces, but he frequently used a distinctive blossom motif in his engraving. Another characteristic of his work was the unique rowel pin detail of silver mounting with a rear projection, and the use of a copper pin against the silver mounting. He often used alternating diagonal strips of copper and brass.

Tom Johnson, Jr. in the doorway of his shop established in 1912 after he left P. M. Kelly's. Unknown assistant on the right.

Few makers used this heart motif in its simplicity as elegantly as Tom Johnson, Jr. Note the identifiable blossom motif engraving detail. Tom Johnson did not mark any of his pieces.

These spurs were presumably made by Tom Johnson, Sr. when in Coleman, Texas. His gal-legs were always flat; another characteristic of his work was the horizontal placement of his decorative card suits on the heel band.
Bob Green collection.

These unmarked spurs are attributed to Tom Johnson, Jr. and were made while in Dalhart, Texas. Contributing to this conclusion is the identifiable rowel pin detail of silver mounting with rear projection, copper pin against silver mounting on which is engraved the traditional blossom motif. This detail is occasionally found on Kelly Bros. pieces which undoubtedly Tom Johnson, Jr. made while working with P.M. Kelly. *Kurt House collection.*

PASCAL M. KELLEY
1886 - 1976

★★★★★	$$$	◆◆
Collectibility	Value	Scarcity

1886	Born in Van Zandt County, Texas; 2 brothers and 4 sisters.
1897	Brother Grady born.
1903	Started making bits and spurs to raise money.
1904	Brother Leo born.
1907	Opened a blacksmith/mechanic shop in Hansford County.
1910	Worked for McChesney in Paul's Valley, OK.
1911	Opened shop with Tom Johnson in Dalhart, TX.
1912	Tom Johnson left; Published first catalog; pieces marked Kelly Bros. Hired Clyde Parker as partner until 1919.
1918	Married Hettie Vititoe with whom he raised 2 boys and 2 girls.
1924	Moved to El Paso, TX.
1930s	Bit and spur business very slow. Building pumps with his Hot Ball Engine.
1935	Moved to Mexico to make engines; brothers managed business in El Paso.
1939	Bought out brothers and resumed El Paso business. Marked pieces "Kelly".
1945	Son Bob joined the business.
1952	Brother Grady died.
1959	Developed Rodeo line of economical bits and spurs.
1965	Sold business to Jim Renalde of Denver, Colo., and moved to Oceanside, Calif., to live with son Jack. Brother Leo died.
1976	Pascal died in California.

An engraved wriggle pattern surrounds each piece of silver overlay on Kelly's pieces. This wriggle engraving also served the purpose of cleaning the excess solder which oozed out while attaching the mounting. He often used an engraved wheat straw pattern. His earlier pieces were more intricate than later ones. Kelly spurs are marked under the spur leather button.

This is the most commonly seen **KELLY BROS** mark. It is called the beveled mark and was used for a period of 20 years between 1919 and 1939. The Kelly Bros marks are noticeably lighter struck than other makers' stamps, usually they are more difficult to read.

P.M. Kelly used this mark KELLY in El Paso, Texas after 1939. Here it is shown on the port of a curb bit. On spurs the mark is below the button on the outside of the heelband. On bits it is also stamped on the outside of the cheekpiece.

This makers mark "+" was used for P.M. Kelly's seconds. These seconds resulted from one spur being made a little longer than its mate, or other non-uniform dimension. Reportedly, there is an "O" mark which denotes the same traits.

P.M. Kelly **PAT'D** the staple swinging button in 1921.

One of the earliest examples of a marked KELLY BROS. spur which was made by Tom Johnson, Jr. when he was the senior partner in Dalhart, Texas.

One of Kelly's favored motifs was the steer head design. This spur is from the O.R. Huff collection.

P.M.Kelly identified this spur as No.70 which is commonly know as the four hearts (three on heelband and one as spur button). These silver engraved hearts are overlaid on a brass background which is overlaid on the iron heel-band. All of this was available for only $9.00 in the early 1900s.

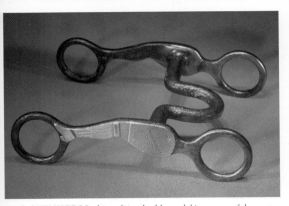

Marked KELLY BROS. this traditional gal-leg curb bit was one of the most popular styles of the Texas bit-and-spur makers.

"THE DEVIL RIVER SPECIAL" two-piece spur with "Marfa" shanks, patented swinging staple button and 1 1/4 inch heelbands with immense six-pointed rowel is one of the largest spurs that Kelly Bros. made with overall length of 7 1/2 inches. Reportedly, these large spurs lost their popularity during the 1920s. Note the silver dollar spur leather conchos. *Ellis Ramsey collection.*

"LA CHEUR SPECIAL" No.216 illustrated in Kelly Bros. catalog No.20. These marked spurs were the most expensive Kelly Bros. spurs made in the mid 1920s selling for $16.00. Ellis Ramsey collection.

Here is an example of a one-piece exceedingly rare Kelly Bros. spur valued in excess of $10,000. These marked **KELLY BROS.** spurs called "HOLLYWOOD SPECIAL" sold originally for $15.00 in the 1920s

Kelly Bros. made a few bits to match specific patterns of spurs. This "HOLLYWOOD SPECIAL" bit is such an example, originally priced at $10.00. Headstall by R.T.Fraizer Pueblo, Colorado. Scott Carter collection.

These spurs represent the most popular singular pattern made by more spur makers than any other spur. It was manufactured and called "JOHNNIE MULLENS SPECIAL" by Kelly Bros, Crockett, McChesney, Buermann, Wallie Boone, Nocona, Powder River, and C.P. Shipley. Some makers spelled the name differently as "JOHNNY MULLINS" and most used the same identifying number or combination of numbers. Johnnie Mullens was a Rodeo star in the 1930's.

Jay Lyndes collection.

In 1959 P.M. Kelly developed a new line of products that could be manufactured at a lower cost yet maintaining the same standard of quality, it was called RODEO. Kelly eliminated the silver mountings, and engraved the steel directly.

This marked **KELLY BROS.** spur is not illustrated in any of the Kelly catalogs, but it is shown in the 1931 Denver Dry Goods catalog as the "POWDER RIVER."

KELLY BROTHERS AND PARKER
1912 - 1919

In 1912, after Tom Johnson left the Kelly business in Dalhart, Texas, Pascal hired Clyde Parker as a partner until 1919. Their pieces during this period were marked K. B. & P.

The partnership of Kelly Bros and Parker marked their pieces with two different stamps. This maker's mark of KELLY BROS & PARKER was not used as frequently as the second mark of K.B.& P. Comparing both K.B.& P. marks and Kelly Bros. it is apparent that the K.B.& P. stamp was more clearly defined.

Extremely rare mark. It is uncertain if this stamp P&KB is associated with the partnership of Kelly Bros. and Parker which were in business in Dalhart, Texas from 1912 to 1919. Only one pair of spurs known with this mark.

Rarely does one see this innovative composition of the Rattlesnake motif which was available in two different patterns as shown. Both of these pairs are marked **K.B.& P.** *L.F. Blake collection.*

Both bits are marked **K.B.& P.** *with similar shield patterns, but detailed differently. Abe Hayes collection.*

K & C 1920s

★★★★★	$$$$	◆◆◆◆
Collectibility	Value	Scarcity

There is a mystery as to the origins of bits and spurs marked K & C. Different points of view on the issue are expressed fully in the discussion of the topic by Bruce Bartlett and Bill Adamson in **Bit and Spur Makers in the Texas Tradition.** Here are a few of the ideas they agree on: K & C spurs were most likely made in the late 1920s. K & C does not stand for Kansas City Saddlery. The K and C probably do stand for Kelley and Crockett. Most examples reflect Kelly Bros. workmanship in both the iron work and the engraving and show little Crockett influence. However the real issue is, Did they ever have a formal partnership? That has not been adequately substantiated, and it is for future generations to uncover some missing link that will clear up the debate.

*It is theorized that Kelly Bros. are responsible for the majority of the pieces marked **K&C**. This marked K&C pair of spurs reflect the Kelly Bros. style. This exact spur style is shown in Kelly Bros. catalog #20, dated 1927, identified as spur No. 214, "POWDER RIVER SPECIAL." Abe Hays collection.*

*This marked **K&C** two-piece gal-leg bit closely resembles pieces made by Kelly Bros.*

There is speculation regarding the origin of this mark; illustrating a possible scenario, this image compares both **K&C** and **K.B&P.** marked pieces.

Engraving detail of heart motif comparing **Kelly Bros.** (left) and **Crockett** (right).
Jay Lyndes collection.

Gal-leg pattern illustrating the differences of engraving **Kelly Bros.** (left) and **K&C** (right). Those pieces marked **K&C** have a closer similarity with the style of **Kelly Bros.** engraving than that of Crockett.

JOHN HENRY KEY
1915 - 2000

★★★	$$	◆◆◆
Collectibility	Value	Scarcity

1915	Born in Liberty County, Texas.
1927	Learned to make spurs from his father.
1930s	Worked for a rancher.
1942	Worked for Humble Pipeline Company.
1948	Made first spurs out of Monel.
1956	Made pieces out of stainless steel.
1982	Retired as a blacksmith.
1996	Exhibit of Key's work in Sam Houston Regional Library in Liberty, Texas.

He preferred to make straight shank or bottle-opener style spurs and made frequent use of both Mexican and American coins as spur leather buttons.

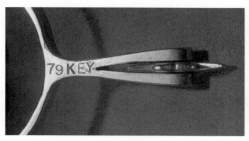

Key marked this spur with his name **KEY** *and date* **79** *on the underside of the shank.*

Key made his spurs of stainless steel without decoration. He used both Mexican and American coins as spur leather buttons. Ronnie Key collection.

M.L. KNOWLTON
1910 - 1996
KNOWLTON BROTHERS
1927 - 1941

★★	$$	◆◆◆◆◆
Collectibility	Value	Scarcity

1910	M.L. born in Borden County, Texas.
1927	Established blacksmith shop with brothers Jack and Buck in Vealmoor, Texas.
1929	Made first spurs at Vealmoor.
1935	Married Velma Smith whose father was a blacksmith.
1938	Moved to Ackerly, Texas.
1941	Volunteered for U.S. Air Force.
1943	Discharged and returned to Ackerly to expand welding business.
1962	Moved to Big Spring, Texas.
1982	Discontinued welding shop; established gunsmithing business.
1996	Died and was buried at Vealmoor, Texas.

Often the customer's initials were placed on his spurs on the bottom side of the shank where it meets the heel band. All spurs were hammered out by hand in classical one-piece construction.

Marked beneath swinging button **KNOWLTON. BRS.** on the outside of one spur and **ACKERLY. TEXAS** on the outside of the other.

Nice pair of cowboy black iron spurs. Wayne Mitchell collection.

JOHN R. KOENIG AND KOENIG BROTHERS
1910 - 1996

★★★	$$$	◆◆◆◆◆
Collectibility	Value	Scarcity

1858	John born in La Grange, Texas.
1881	Married Mrs. Minna Meyer.
1900	Operating blacksmith shop in La Grange.
1913	His wife, Minna, died; he retired as a blacksmith.
1921	Married Anna Eckel.
1936	Died in La Grange.

Koenig spurs are not marked by the maker. His spurs can be described as "dainty" with narrow heel bands and a short, straight shank. The silver mountings are both overlaid and inlaid.

These spurs are not marked but attributed to Koenig.

Ewell Julius Kohler
1906 - 1981

★★	$$$	◆◆◆◆◆
Collectibility	Value	Scarcity

1906	Born on family ranch near Boise City, Oklahoma.
1919	Moved to Arkansas.
1930	Returned to ranch with wife, Parlee. Worked in blacksmith shop on ranch making bits and spurs.
1981	Died of cancer.

Ewell forged one-piece spurs with simple, but interesting designs.

JULIUS KUNSHICK
1892 - 1966

His simply designed one-piece spurs were not marked. They were made with narrow heel bands in the lightweight, East Texas style with small fine-pointed rowels. He was known to use gold overlays on his pieces, which was unusual among Texas makers.

KYLE-PETTIGREW-MOORE

★★	$$	◆◆◆
Collectibility	Value	Scarcity

Fred D. Kyle, Jr. 1934 - 1995
Kenneth Moore 1920s - 1980s
Eugene Pettigrew 1930s -

Fred D. Kyle, Jr.

1960	Kyle Machine Works established.
1965	Ken Moore financed the manufacture of 12 spur styles.
1968	Moore ended the partnership with Kyle. Gene Pettigrew and Fred Kyle became partners.
1970	Pettigrew left the partnership. Kyle Products began producing bits.
1975	Kyle Products stopped making bits and spurs.
1982	Kyle Machine Works ended and became Tool Traders with the Kyle sons, Robert and David involved in production until 1995 when Fred died and the company closed.

The partnership of Kyle, Pettigrew, and Moore marked their pieces in different ways depending on who was working together at a specific time. The first partnership was

Moore and Kyle who marked their spurs **MOORE** under the swinging button.

The second mark was **MP** (inside a spur shape) as shown beneath the button.

The last pieces manufactured were stamped **KYLE** below the spur leather button.

The next mark was **KP** (backward K with a P inside a circle) next to the swinging button.

These spurs which are marked **MP** with wide heelbands, swinging sloping buttons, and small rowels are characteristic of this partnership.
Wayne Mitchell collection.

FRANK. L. LONGTINE
1911 - 1982

★★	$$	◆◆◆◆◆
Collectibility	Value	Scarcity

1911	Born in Leydon, North Dakota.
1922	Mother died, Father ill with TB; went to live with uncle.
1924	Father died; Frank ran away; worked his way to Waco, Texas. Cowboyed in Texas, Colorado, Nevada, Oregon and Montana.
1931	Made his first spurs.
1933	Married Effie Johnson in Montana. Started silver engraving.
1936	Moved to Lander, WY with family; cowboying.
1942	Working as metals collector for war effort.
1946	Wife and children left him and returned to MT.
1951	Married Ruth Elaine Bell in Riverton, WY. Worked for Atlantic Richfield Oil Co. until retirement.
1960s	Made buckles and spurs for the rodeo in Riverton.
1970s	Had several heart attacks.
1982	Died in Lander hospital.

Frank also made and repaired guns decorated with silver and also saddles.

Few examples of Longtine spurs exist. These silver-mounted spurs are decorated with copper Liberty pennies, silver engraved heart and diamond motifs.
Max Longtine collection.

Longtine marked this engraved silver overlaid bit **FL** on the slobber bar. This bit reflects the influence of the early Vaquero style bits of California and Nevada.
Max Longtine collection

LUCIO MANRIQUEZ
1904 - 1976

★★★★	$$$	◆◆◆◆◆
Collectibility	Value	Scarcity

1904	Born in Shafter, Texas, one of 8 children.
1930	Worked at a silver mine as blacksmith and mechanic for 12 years.
1942	Mine closed. Stayed on as private contractor.
1943	Worked at Fowlks Brothers Ranch near Alpine, Texas as ranch blacksmith until 1958.
1958	Worked as blacksmith in shop of Cy Pheffer in Saragosa, Texas, until 1969.
1969	Moved back to Shafter and made bits and spurs in shop outside of his home.
1976	Died of a heart attack.

Manriquez was one of the few Texas makers who would inlay copper or silver on his spurs and liked to mix copper, silver and brass on his mountings. He is said to have originated the "Marfa shank" on his spurs. This deeply curved shank design was a characteristic of his spurs.

Manriquez is said to be the originator of the "Marfa Shank" which is shown in each of these images of his spurs. Here Manriquez has used the combination of copper, brass and silver mountings depicting a card suit motif.

This little-known but important maker has used Mexican coins as a decorative element both on the heelbands as well as the spur leather buttons.
(above) Bruce Bartlett collection; (below) Brock Walden collection.

JOHN ROBERT MCCHESNEY
1868 - 1928

★★★★★	$$$	◆◆
Collectibility	Value	Scarcity

1868	Born in Plymouth, Marshall County, Indiana.
1884	Moved to Asher, Arkansas, where John married Tobitha.
1886	Moved with wife to Broken Arrow in Indian Territory.
1890	Moved to Gainesville, Texas.
1896	Active bit-and-spur making business in Gainesville.
1906	First catalog issued.
1909	Moved to Pauls Valley, Oklahoma, and opened J.R. McChesney Spur and Bit Company with 50 employees and a large mail order business.
1920	Tried new businesses: auto repair, hotel and excursion boats.
1928	Died of a heart attack. Business sold to Nocona Boot Co.
1955	McChesney equipment was acquired by Adolph Bayers.

McChesney popularized the three-dimensional trumpet vine motif on his spurs. Another characteristic pattern of his was the peacock with or without jewels in his tail. He always offered the option of the patented Olmstead locking rowel on his spurs. The majority of his spurs had narrow heel bands seldom exceeding 5/8 of an inch in width. He offered a wide range of options with each single spur style. An identifying characteristic of McChesney's early pieces was the application of the twisted copper and brass wire detail on his spurs.

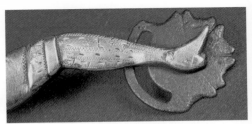

The Olmstead lock web rowel was available for all of McChesney's spurs at an additional cost of 50¢. *Lawson and Nancy Waldon collection.*

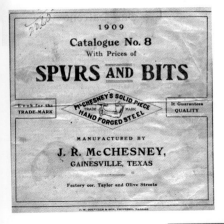

1909
Catalogue No. 8
With Prices of

SPURS AND BITS

Look for this
TRADE-MARK

Mc CHESNEY'S SOLID PIECE
TRADE · MARK
HAND FORGED STEEL

It Guarantees
QUALITY

MANUFACTURED BY

J. R. McCHESNEY,
GAINESVILLE, TEXAS

Factory cor. Taylor and Olive Streets

J. W. COLVILLE & SON, PRINTERS, DALLAS.

McChesney's trademark as illustrated on the cover of his Catalog #8 dated 1909 Gainesville, Texas, was an arm & hammer stamp. J.R. McChesney was making bits and spurs close to forty years without marking his pieces except for this logo of the arm & hammer which appears only on few early pieces. *Sonny Parsons collection.*

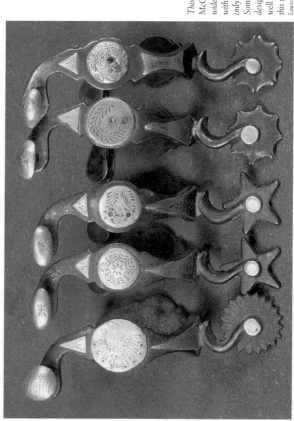

This selection of five different mountings on McChesney's spur style No. 19 illustrates the wide range of options that were available with a single spur style. McChesney was the only Texas bit-and-spur maker to do this. Some of the innovative compositions of rowel designs by this important maker are shown as well as the unusual shaped spur button on this up-turned heelband.

Lawson and Nancy Walden collection.

These custom-ordered double- mounted spurs with a decorative treatment of steer head motif, and shield pattern creates a striking design on these silvered gal-leg spurs with gold slippers. Charles Forbes collection.

Beautifully stylized, this Flamingo bit with copper legs, silver body, and gold beak exemplifies McChesney's innovative designs.

125

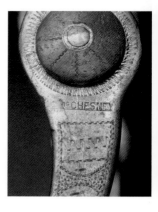

It was not until McChesney's business was sold to the Justin-Nocona Boot Co. in 1928 that they began marking their bits and spurs **McCHESNEY**, *using three different sized stamps. The earliest mark was the largest stamp: 1/4-inch letters stamped inside the heelband. Followed by 1/8 inch letters stamped outside under the button. The last mark used had 1/16-inch letters stamped under the button, and the bits were marked on the outside of the cheek.*

Marked **McCHESNEY** with 1/16-inch letters this bit
was made by Nocona Boot Co.

This is the quintessential McChesney spur. Copper gal-leg shank with
Olmstead patented locking rowel, and the classic three-dimensional trumpet
vine motif which McChesney popularized. *Lawson and Nancy Waldon collection.*

Jesus Morales
1888 - 1965

★★★★	$$$	◆◆◆◆◆
Collectibility	Value	Scarcity

1888	Born in Mexico and trained there as a blacksmith.
1918	Farrier for U.S. Army Cavalry in Los Angeles, Texas.
1927	Settled in Cotulla, Texas.
1965	Killed by a drunk driver as he crossed the street in Cotulla, Texas.

Morales did not mark his work. He made most of his tools, but did not even own a hammer. He was seen using a monkey wrench as a hammer. He forged one-piece spurs and one-piece bits out of old Model T or Model A axles.

These Morales spurs were custom-made for Roy Hindes.

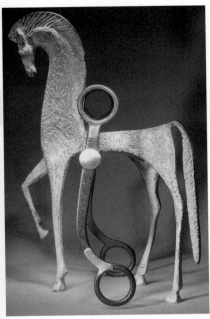

Texas style bit with unusually long cheekpieces, and minimal mountings.

These iron spurs which show some good honest cowboy wear are attributed to Morales who did not mark his work.
Ernie Davis collection.

Joseph Johnson Nance
1870 - 1947

★★★★	$$$$	◆◆◆◆◆
Collectibility	Value	Scarcity

1870	Born in Bee County, Texas.
1896	Married and moved to Ozona, in Crockett County, Texas.
1900	Opened his first blacksmith shop.
1907	Moved to ranch in Terrell County.
1911	Sold ranch and moved to Sanderson, Texas.
1914-1915	Nance & Sons listed in Business Directory in Lometa, TX.
1918-1929	Elected sheriff of Terrell County.
1930s	Built and operated Loma Alta Tourist Camp.
1947	Died.

Nance made very delicate bits, but built a heavy spur with wide heel bands.

*This maker's mark **JOE NANCE** is stamped with individual letters on the port of a bit.*

Occasionally a maker known for his delicately made bits, built a heavier heel-band style of spur as shown. *James Haley collection.*

Classic Texas-style grazing bit marked **JOE NANCE**. *This short-cheeked two-piece bit was favored by Texas cowboys. An unexplainable fact is that Crockett offered this style of bit in his Catalog #12 as the NANCE BIT No.142 for $5.00.* *James Haley collection.*

NORTH & JUDD MANUFACTURING CO.

1863 - PRESENT

★ Collectibility	$ Value	◆ Scarcity

1832	North Company making saddlery hardware.
1863	Firm incorporated as North & Judd Mfg. Co.
1878	Began using an anchor stamp to mark pieces.
1900	Employed 500 people.
1926	Purchased Buermann Mfg. Co.
1950s	Scaled down bit and spur production.

MAIN PLANT AT NEW BRITAIN, CONN. (1940)

This Eureka spur was made by North & Judd and illustrated in price list dated 1886-7 as No.3 Plain. It was embossed with a large **ANCHOR***, the trademark for the company. In later years a small anchor was stamped inside the heelband. North & Judd offered this same spur until 1947. The original Eureka spurs were patented by A. Buermann and advertised in 1876.*

132

This Mexican-style spur was manufactured in the eastern states in 1865 by Russell & Erwin Mfg. Co. Both North & Judd, and A. Buermann made this spur with identical Nos.1244 as shown in their catalogs. They identified this spur first as Mexican, then Californian, then Texas and finally as South American style, without any physical change to the spur.

Marked **STAR STEEL SILVER**, these spurs were identified as No.1044 by North & Judd (1940s) with chased steerhead motif. N.&J. was cultivating the same markets as P.M. Kelly (1959) with his new "rodeo" line of chasing on plain iron with no mountings. Perhaps Kelly was influenced by N.&J. with this new technique. This alloy was also used by A. Buermann as well as the Hercules Bronze for manufacturing bits and spurs. *Ralph Emerson collection.*

JOSEPH CARL PETMECKY
1840 - 1929

★★★★★	$$$$$	◆◆◆◆◆
Collectibility	Value	Scarcity

1840	Born in Weisbaden, Germany.
1845	Emigrated with family to New Braunfels, Texas.
1851	Joe went to Austin to find work.
1856	Opened a gunsmith shop in Austin.
1860	Closed shop and fought in the Confederate Army.
1865	Reopened shop in Austin and married Adolphina.
1870s	Returned to gunsmithing.
1872	Introduced a new lightweight spur.
1920	Became semi-retired.
1929	Died in Austin.

Petmecky marked some of his early spurs with the same stamped name that was applied to his guns. This early Texas gunsmith conceived the idea of producing a lightweight spur in marked contrast to the heavy Mexican Chihuahua style that the Texas vaqueros were wearing prior to the Civil War. Petmecky was the first Texas maker to use thin gauge tempered steel for his heel bands. He often embellished his spurs with inlaid brass or copper. The early spurs made by Petmecky in the 1870s with the curved shank later became one of the most popular styles of spur known. They were manufactured and widely marketed by Buermann as the OK spur.

Petmecky was the first Texas maker to use thin gauge tempered steel for his heelbands. His formal training as a gunsmith influenced his selection of these materials.
Steve Wilson collection.

These significant spurs first made and marked **J.C. PETMECKY** in the 1870s later became one of the most popular styles of spur known. It took A. Buermann's manufacturing genius and marketing skills to offer his O.K. spur to every cowboy in America at the price of 65 cents a pair, a price they could afford.

*These consummate gal-leg spurs are attributed to one of the earliest Texas makers J.C. Petmecky. Seldom seen are these delicate copper inlaid saw-tooth rowels, a departure from the early massive Mexican rowel. **AUSTIN TEXAS** is engraved on the silver mountings on both spurs.*
Ellis Ramsey collection.

Powder River and Denver Dry Goods Co.

by Bill Adamson

★★★★★	$$$$	◆◆◆◆◆
Collectibility	Value	Scarcity

1894	McNamara's Dry Goods renamed The Denver Dry Goods Co.
1907	DDGCo. builds six-story city-block-size building.
1920	Frank E. Newhagen (1886-1951) to form "Stockmen's Store" dept.
1920's	Newhagen builds dept. and catalog sales, using White & Davis model.
1927	Catalog features Kelly Bros. and North & Judd.
1930	Starts own brand of saddles, "POWDER RIVER".
1934	Adopts house brand "POWDER RIVER" for bits and spurs.
1936	Erosion begins on "POWDER RIVER" brand; Crockett back in catalog.
1940	Adopts Renalde as a prelude to DON RICARDO. Crockett, Powder River in decline.
1941	DON RICARDO replaces Renalde; Powder River out for bits and spurs.

Powder River brand spurs were produced during the 1930s by Kelly Bros. Their heyday was 1934 to 1936 when they were sold exclusively by Denver Dry Goods Company. Because they were only lightly stamped (like the Kelly Bros. mark), with a little rust, the mark could be overlooked.

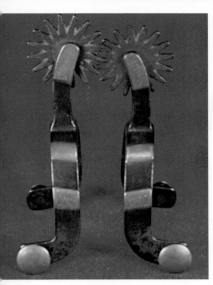

Powder River brand No.91-L, "THE POWDER RIVER" another Kelly Bros. rendition, ca. 1934-36, possibly a little later. *Leyton Yearout collection.*

Special order version of the No.91-1044, "COLORADO" style. One can immediately see the Kelly Bros. rendition of a typical Powder River spur ca. 1934-36. *Scott Carter collection*

137

PRISON BITS AND SPURS IN HUNTSVILLE, TEXAS

★★★	$$$	◆◆◆
Collectibility	Value	Scarcity

1849	Huntsville prison opened.
1865	It was the only Confederate prison still standing after the Civil War.
1910	First known pair of prison-made spurs.
1931	Prison rodeo established so increased spur production.

Bits and spurs made by prison inmates varied widely in their creativity and craftsmanship. One characteristic often seen was the use of abalone or mother-of-pearl as a decorative addition. Sometimes plastics might be used for a spot of color.

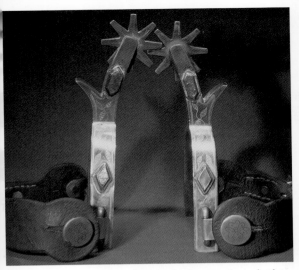

Chased floral pattern on stainless steel abalone bezel settings. Accented with brass-tipped chap guard, shanks, and engraved brass rowels, these spurs reflect the creativity of this unknown prison maker. Frank Loftin collection.

Early example of Huntsville Prison black iron forged spurs. Innovative rowel design using a drill press to create this pattern. Reportedly made for Judge A.W. Sagert ca.1910. Calvin Patrick collection.

These dainty prison spurs were reportedly made from a 1930s woman's purse handle. A distinguishing characteristic of Huntsville prison spurs are the beautifully detailed ornate rowels with points shaped like boots.
Coryell Museum and Historical Center.

An example of stainless steel spurs with brass overlaid arrow motif. Decorated with abalone and red plastic (from inmate's tooth brush) make an innovative composition. *Douglas Diehl collection.*

This elaborately embellished spur with mother of pearl in heart and diamond settings is complimented by this exquisitely detailed rowel with cowboy boot shapes. *Calvin Patrick collection.*

RENALDE MANUFACTURING COMPANY BY BILL ADAMSON
1938 - 1978

★ Collectibility	$ Value	◆◆ Scarcity

1927	Denver Metals Foundry, founded by James Renalde, Sr.	**JAMES RENALDE, SR.** 1897 - 1991
1938	Began production of aluminum bits and spurs.	**JAMES JR.** 1922 - 1987
1951	Announced purchase of Crockett Bit and Spur Co.	
1953	Crockett Cat.#53; greetings from Renalde, adds saddle hardware, buckles.	
1965	Acquired Kelly and Sons; now Renalde, Crockett and Kelly.	
1966	Produced 200,000 bits, spurs and pieces of saddle hardwear a year.	
1973	Reorganization; Crockett and Kelly, by Renalde.	
1977	Receivership; Hank Kugeler and Bob Harrison new owners, managers.	
1980	Dropped Renalde name; Horsts new owners of Crockett and Kelly, Inc.	

James Renalde started making aluminum bits and spurs in 1938 and continued to produce these through World War II. He acquired the Crockett line of bits and spurs in 1951 and finally purchased Kelly & Sons in 1965 becoming the world's largest producer of bits, spurs and saddlery hardware. This family-owned company dominated the market for about twenty years until the 1970s when James Renalde, Sr. died and the firm changed hands and gradually went out of business.

Makers mark of **C-R** (Crockett-Renalde) within a horseshoe on stainless swinger. This mark was employed from 1953-77, used in various locations, came to be standard on the spur leather button swinger in the latter half of the period.

Script **R** mark used in the "Renalde, Crockett, Kelly" 1974-78 period.

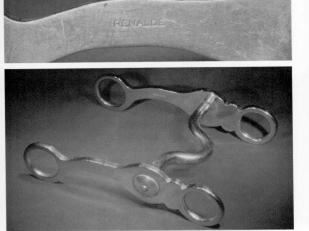

Aluminum bit No.705 marked **RENALDE** inside of cheek-piece. This was available either engraved or plain circa 1938-50.

Ricardo Metal Manufacturers
by Bill Adamson
1941 - 1973

★ Collectibility	$ Value	◆◆ Scarcity

Ed (Frank Edward) Newhagen, Jr. 1916 - 1963

1940 RICARDO was the brainchild of Frank Edward Newhagen, Sr.

1941 DON RICARDO aluminum bits and spurs are in Denver Dry Goods catalog.

1943 Expanded line includes plain steel, nickel-plated steel, sterling mountings.

1947 Added nickel-silver bits and spurs, sterling mounted, script Ricardo.

1950 Seventeen employees, broad product line.

1951 Frank Newhagen dies.

1954 Ed Newhagen is owner/operator of Ricardo Metal Manufacturers.

1963 Ed Newhagen dies; wife Catherine assumes control.

1966 Jack A. Weil, President and new owner.

1971 Houston interests buy the company, move it to Victoria, TX.

1973 Company operation ceases.

Ricardo replaced Renalde as the main producer of bits and spurs in the 1941 Denver Dry Goods Co. catalog making minor changes to the Renalde bit line and no changes to the spur line except the name change. To the Ricardo aluminum products made by Renalde, Ricardo added a line of plated-steel bits and spurs, mounted, using a model obtained from Crockett, numerous models built by Kelly, and some by Renalde.

During the forties and fifties, Ricardo was rapidly adding product line. They were virtually the sole domestic source for Denver Dry's needs for bits, spurs and buckles, and Ricardo had attracted a wide following among celebrities and groups and foreigners.

These marked **DON RICARDO** *"Nickel Steel" spurs with aluminum rowels were available plain as shown or engraved. Nickel Steel was an alloy of steel and nickel similar to monel. It was used by Ricardo 1946-1948.* George Brown collection.

Maker's mark in script Ricardo *introduced 1947 on "Nickel Silver" line. nickel silver (also known as German Silver) has no silver in it. Made of copper and nickel, it is more durable than sterling or coin silver.*

Ricardo bit "The Santa Barbara" was available with choice of three mouthpieces, Nickel Silver with Sterling Silver mountings, their most expensive bit, produced only 1947-48. Wheat Collection, Ranching Heritage Assn., Lubbock, Texas

ADOLPH FRANK SCHNEIDER
1871 - 1949

★★★	$$$	◆◆◆◆◆
Collectibility	Value	Scarcity

1871	Born at Fredericksburg, Texas.
1910	Married Sophie Mueller Lisette. Daughter Elise born.
1915	Fell from windmill; permanently disabled.
1917	Daughter Dora born.
1920	Moved to Menard; established blacksmith shop.
1949	Died in Brady, Texas.

Schneider did not mark his pieces. Both his bits and spurs were lightly-built and distinctive in the East-Texas style. Both bits and spurs often bear the distinctive two small diamond-shaped mountings. Apparently made of spring or lightly-forged steel, they resemble both McChesney and more so the maker Petmecky in striking ways.

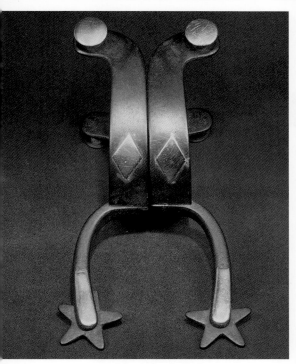

Unmarked spurs attributed to Adolf Schneider. Bill Swope collection.

Schneider did not mark his bits. Bill Swope collection.

CLAY SHEARER
1890 - 1968

1890	Born with the name McClay in Clay County, Texas.
1901	Moved to Uvalde County in horse drawn covered wagons.
1905	Moved to Batesville, Texas.
1907	Built blacksmith shop on the square in Batesville.
1911	Moved to La Pryor, in Zavala County, TX.
1917	Served in U.S. Army in W.W.I.
1921	Married Jessie Adams.
1928	Opened business in Crystal City, Zavala County.
1939	Patented cattle squeeze chute.
1940	Formed partnership and later sold company to A. C. Mogford.
1961	Suffered paralytic stroke.
1968	Died in Batesville, Texas; buried in Fort Sam Houston, San Antonio, TX.

Shearer would make whatever style the customer ordered: wide heel bands or narrow. He frequently used Mexican coins as decorative elements, and his silver mountings were seldom engraved.

He created a locking rowel spur with a pin hinged on the chap guard which falls into place, thus preventing the rowel from spinning.

Shearer did not mark his bits or spurs.

This little-known maker had exceptional mechanical abilities. He created this locking rowel spur with a pin hinged on the chap guard which falls into place, thus preventing the rowel from spinning.
Sonny Parsons collection

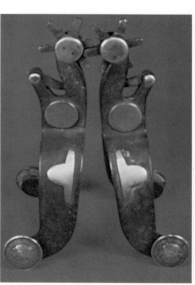

Shearer would make whatever style the customer ordered, wide heelbands or narrow. He frequently used Mexican coins as decorative elements. His silver mountings were seldom engraved.
Sonny Parsons collection

SHIPLEY SADDLERY AND MERCANTILE CO. 1885 - 1972
CHARLES P. SHIPLEY
1864 - 1943

★★★★★	$$$$$	♦♦♦♦
Collectibility	Value	Scarcity

1864	Charles P. Shipley born in Wooster, Ohio.
1885	Opened Saddlery in Kansas City, Missouri.
1910	Shipley Saddlery incorporated and built a three-story building.
1911	Son Clyde working as vice-president and sales manager.
1912	First C. P. Shipley Catalog #12 published.
1915	Bought G.A. Bischoff's company.
1916	Bought Oscar Crockett's C & G line, catalog, and tools.
1920	Crockett bought bit and spur department back from Shipley.
1940	Charles Shipley had a stroke and Clyde took over.
1943	Charles Shipley died.
1952	Clyde died of colon cancer.
1953	Clyde's son Charles P. Shipley II ran the business until it closed in 1972.

One of the earliest and most successful businesses of its kind, Shipley Saddlery played a prominent part in the growth and prosperity of Kansas City. Some of Shipley's pieces were supplied by other manufacturers of bits and spurs (Buermann, Bischoff, McChesney and O. Crockett). However all pieces, regardless of the maker, were clearly marked C. P. Shipley. One of the distinguishing characteristics of Shipley spurs is the wrap-around silver overlaid buttons, which were always fixed buttons.

Shipley marked his pieces in a clear and precise manner. His spurs were marked **C.P. SHIPLEY** inside the heelband on one spur and **KAN. CITY MO.** on the other inside of the same spur.

Some of Shipley's pieces were supplied by other manufactures of bits and spurs. This piece made by August Buermann Mfg. Co. for C.P. Shipley is marked **C.P. SHIPLEY**.

One of the distinguishing characteristics of Shipley spurs is the wrap-around silver overlaid buttons. Shipley spurs always had fixed spur leather buttons.
Jim Williams collection.

151

These three single spurs are marked **C.P. SHIPLEY** *but made by other makers (right to Left: G.A. Bischoff, O.Crockett, and August Buermann) illustrating that other makers supplied Shipley. Ellis Ramsey collection.*

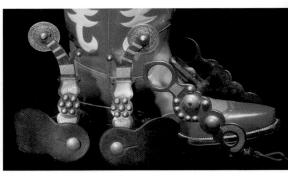

Seldom does one find a silver inlaid bit or spur stamped with a Texas maker's mark. These handsomely-crafted pieces are marked **C.P. SHIPLEY**. *It is known that Buermann made bits and spurs for Shipley, and these appear to be an example. Shipley offered inlaid spurs as illustrated in his catalog No.28; this is only the third pair known to exist. Note use of unusual Mexican coin rowel.*
Jim Williams collection.

This classic double gal-leg pattern mounted with engraved copper and silver is elegant in its simplicity. Ellis Ramsey collection.

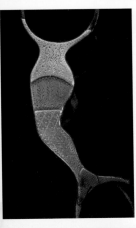

Exquisitely engraved, this gal-leg bit exemplifies superior craftmanship.
Jim Williams collection.

Not shown in Shipley's catalogs, this marked **C.P. SHIPLEY** *bit was likely made by Bischoff according to its identifiable patterns and engraving.*

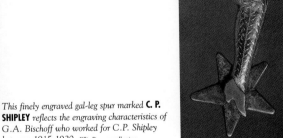

This finely engraved gal-leg spur marked **C. P. SHIPLEY** *reflects the engraving characteristics of G.A. Bischoff who worked for C.P. Shipley between 1915-1920.* Ellis Ramsey collection.

EARLON SHIRLEY
1931 - 2000

★★★	$$$	◆◆
Collectibility	Value	Scarcity

1931	Born at home on a ranch in Dulo, Oklahoma.
1948	Working in a cotton gin in Mayfield, OK. Married Joyce when both were 17.
1950	Living in Border, TX when first daughter born.
1950s	Started making silver jewelry as a hobby.
1967	Started making bits and spurs in Memphis, Texas, at home when not managing the cotton gin there. He made mostly spurs and knives, only a few bits.
1979	Moved to Tahoca, Texas and managed the cotton gin there. Made spurs for the ranch rodeo at Abilene.
1997	Moved back to Erick, OK when he retired and was diagnosed with Lou Gehrig's disease.
2000	Died of ALS.

Earlon never owned a horse and didn't wear spurs, but he enjoyed making them for others. He prided himself on making good working spurs of the best materials available with a high polish on them. He made both dainty small-banded ones and some with large heel bands. He marked them with a gang stamp with his name in script and a serial number. For a long time he made one-piece spurs and later made two piece spurs welded with a wire welder. He was a member of the International Spur Makers Guild.

154

Double-mounted Shirley spurs with overlaid silver designs, initials, and four 6s for the large ranch of that name in Texas. Marked No. 181. Ben Walker collection

Double gal-leg spurs overlaid with silver and accented with 14K gold. Heart buttons and engraved buckles. Marked No. 2. Jim Butler collection.

Silver overlaid buffalo adorn these spurs marked No. 13 by Shirley.
Ron Tollison collection.

Glen F. "Red" Skelton
1915 - 1996

★★★	$$	◆◆◆◆◆
Collectibility	Value	Scarcity

1915	Born in San Saba County, Texas.
1931	Moved to Channing; cowboying on ranches.
1941	In Army with horse cavalry.
1945	Learned saddlemaking in Phoenix, AZ. Returned to Channing and married Alice.
1946	Working as heavy equipment operator for county and making bits and spurs in spare time.
1985	Retired to make bits and spurs.
1996	Died of lung cancer in Channing, Texas.

Skelton used overlays of copper, brass and silver on his spurs. He marked his pieces with a punch dot: spurs on top of the shank and bits on the port of the mouthpiece.

Red's personal bit. *Alice Skelton collection.*

These spurs Red made for himself. They are one-piece, double-mounted with his name in silver.
Alice Skelton collection.

On occasion a maker is asked to make a spur to match a lost original. Here Skelton matched the missing Isaac Stephenson shown as the horizontal spur.
Ken Miller collection.

ALFRED N. SMITH
1885 - 1954

★★★★	$$$	♦♦♦♦♦
Collectibility	Value	Scarcity

1885	Born in Mound City, Kansas.
1894	Moved with family to Harrisburg, Texas.
1917	Boarding with parents, blacksmithing in father's shop.
1922 -1948	Working in blacksmith shop at 8014 Cypress in Harrisburg.
1954	Died of heart attack.

Although Smith did not mark his spurs or his bits, the style is easily recognizable: his spurs had characteristically narrow heel bands of 1/4 to 1/2 inch in width, sometimes with silver mountings along the entire length. Smith always used flat American silver coins as conchos on his bits.

Smith's spurs had characteristically narrow heelbands, sometimes with silver mountings along the entire length. *Kurt House collection.*

The silver mountings on this one-piece spur by Smith are masterful designs of serrated diamond shapes, and engraved scrolls with gold overlay.
Dwight Huber collection

ISAAC LINDSEY STEPHENSON
1887 - 1953

★★★★	$$$	◆◆◆◆◆
Collectibility	Value	Scarcity

1887	Born in Hall County, Texas.
1901	Moved with parents to Lipscomb County and worked on family farm with his father.
1906	Spent several years as a cowboy in New Mexico, Utah, Nevada, Wyoming and Montana. Learned to make bits and spurs, lariats, cinches and quirts.
1913	Returned to family farm.
1914	Enrolled in mechanical school in Kansas City.
1916	Served in World War I in San Antonio breaking horses for the U.S. Government.
1919	Married Fannie Davis. Lived south of Darrouzett.
1920s	Farming and running repair shop for cars and farm equipment.
1930s	Expanded repair shop and moved it to Darrouzett.
1946	Moved to home he built in Darrouzett. Continued farming and designing and building equipment.
1953	Died in Darrouzett.

Stephenson used combinations of silver, copper and brass overlays. The leading edge of his swinging buttons were cut on a 45° angle. His pieces were marked under the buttons with his initials I.L.S. and a number indicating the style of spur. Another identifying characteristic of Stephenson's spurs is the tapered swinging spur leather button hangers. His spurs usually had a heart-shaped spur leather button on the outside and a round button on the offside.

Stephenson marked his spurs and bits with his initials **I.L.S.** and a number indicating the style of spur. Another identifying characteristic of Stephenson's spurs is the tapered swinging spur leather button hangers.

These magnificent double-mounted one-piece spurs exemplify Stephenson's engraving skills on silver and copper. Note this distinctive dendritic tree laden with fruit as shown with copper inlaid motif, and Stevenson's exaggerated chap guards. *Panhandle Plains Historical Museum.*

Gal-leg spur with rocker-engraved rowels. The heart button is detailed with copper inlaid on a silver background. Of the known Stevenson spurs all have the heart shaped spur leather button on the outside and a round button on the inside. Note the unusual use of a chap guard on a gal-leg spur. Dwight Huber collection

This gal-leg bit of unusual proportion demonstrates Stephenson's creative abilities. Both the half-breed mouthpiece, and slobber bar are departures from the traditional Texas curb bit.

Harold "Swede" Strong
1887 - 1970

★★★★★	$$$$$	◆◆◆◆◆
Collectibility	Value	Scarcity

1887	Born in Sweden.
1902	Left home after mother's death and sailed to New York.
1910	Worked as a stone mason with company that built the capitol in Austin, Texas.
1914	Learned blacksmithing in Army during WW I.
1918	Hired as a cowboy on Loving Ranch, near Rotan, Texas.
1934 -1966	He operated the Pecos Saddle Shop and was more famous for his leather work than his blacksmithing. He won prizes for the saddles he made.

Strong marked his pieces with the logo of a flying S stamped into the iron. Occasionally he stamped a date to accompany his mark. He frequently used the Marfa shank on his spurs.

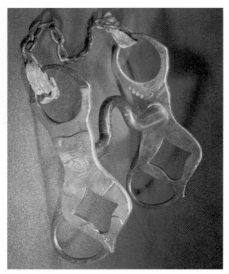

This bit with a double gal-leg pattern ornamented with copper and silver on the cheekpiece matches the spurs shown below This bit is marked with the **flying S** and dated **1928**. There are very few examples of a full-bodied lady bit made by Texas makers. *Wheat collection, the Ranching Heritage Assn.*

This important maker marked most pieces with his logo of a **flying S** stamped into the iron. Occasionally he stamped a date to accompany his mark.

Strong's unusual chased-iron motifs are portrayed with images of "the cowboy sins" wine glass, playing cards, woman's shoe and dice on these spurs. His **flying S** logo is seen at the bottom of the heelband.
Wheat collection, Ranching Heritage Center, Lubbock, TX

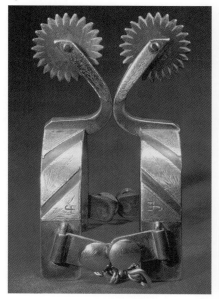

Strong's spurs were made with swinging buttons. The **JW** stamp which is shown on the heelbands denotes these were from the James Wheat collection. Wheat stamped the pieces in his collection profusely to establish his ownership.

165

JULIUS CAESAR STUDER
1863 - 1957

★★	$$	◆◆◆◆◆
Collectibility	Value	Scarcity

1863	Born near Berne, Switzerland.
1865	Came to America; lived in Swiss Colony in Tennessee.
1873	Worked for Banks family doing odd jobs.
1876	Apprentice carriage maker.
1885	Moved to Kiowa, KS; worked as a blacksmith.
1886	Filed on 640 acres in Lipscomb County, TX with five other men.
1887	Moved to Canadian, TX. Making bits and spurs and guns. In grain and livery stable business.
1890	Married Ellie Gallaher at Canadian. They raised six sons and a daughter.
1900	Founder and charter member of Panhandle and Southwestern Livestock Association.
1907 -1916	Maintaining Anvil Park Ranch, grocery stores, packing house, lumber yards and ice factories.
1922	Founded Anvil Park Rodeo. Raised Hereford cattle and some Brahmas for rodeo.
1930s	Organized Rodeo Cowboys Association.
1950	Retired from ranching.
1957	Died; buried in Canadian.

Studer did not make many bits or spurs. He was a very active entrepreneur in Canadian, Texas, where he ran many successful businesses.

Extremely rare mark of this early West Texas blacksmith. Robert Vincent collection.

This marked **J.C. STUDER** *bit has remained in one family's ownership for over 100 years. It belonged to John Thomas Crawford who arrived in the Texas Panhandle in the 1880s and worked as a cowboy on several of the early ranches. In 1902 John Crawford was elected the first sheriff of Gray County.* Robert Vincent collection.

Sylvester "Bull" Thomas
1882 - 1950

★★★		$$		◆◆◆◆
Collectibility		Value		Scarcity

1882	Born March 15.
1930s	Working in local blacksmith shops in Lockridge, then Sandy Point, TX.
1940s	Moved to Rosharon, Texas.
1950	Died at home of a stroke.

His spurs were neither marked, mounted, nor engraved. He was influenced by Bianchi in his preference for the bottle-opener style.

Thomas did not mark his pieces, nor did he use any silver mountings on his spurs. Les Myers collection

Louie "Cowboy" Traylor

1893 - 1972

1893	Born June 18 in Camp County, Texas.
1913	Married Irene Herd.
1914 -1919	Three children born.
1924	December, Incarcerated in Texas State Prison.
1925	Paroled.
1929	Incarcerated in Texas State Prison.
1930	Paroled in August.
1931	Living in Angleton, Brazoria County, Texas. Moved to Rosharon, Texas. Opened blacksmith shop at Sandy Point, Texas.
1940	Moved blacksmith shop to Houston, Texas.
1972	Died in Houston, buried in Pittsburg, Camp County, Texas.

Monel spurs with quarters for buttons. Wheat collection, the Ranching Heritage Assn.

Traylor was one of the first makers to use monel for his spurs. Later he used stainless steel without decoration. His buttons were American coins, usually standing Liberty quarters, and Mercury dimes.

Unmarked spurs with a full silver overlay and coin buttons dated 1920.
Kurt House collection

169

FRED TUCKER
1908 - 2001

★★★	$$
Collectibility	Value
◆◆◆◆◆	
Scarcity	

1908	Born on ranch north of Kenton, Oklahoma.
1911	Fred's mother died; raised by grandparents.
1923	Left school to work on family ranch with father and brother.
1930s	Working in shop on family ranch; Repaired machinery.
1942	Married Eva Nellie Crystal Bressie. Served in the Army for 6 mos. at Fort Benning, Georgia.
1943	Returned to work on the ranch when his father died. Making bits and spurs in the ranch shop.
1990s	Stopped working on the ranch due to poor health.
2001	Died in a nursing home.

It is very unusual to use enamel on spurs. These colorful one-of-a-kind spurs were made in commemoration of the 1976 bicentennial. Few makers attempted to make a miniature as detailed as this example. These personalized spurs with twisted shanks are a splendid example of Tucker's skill. This miniature spur is an exact copy with bone inlaid swinging buttons and a rowel that turns.

Enameled spurs made to commemorate the 1976 bicentennial. *Ken Miller collection.*

These twisted shank, personalized spurs are copied exactly in the tiny miniature without the mountings. The miniature measures 1-1/2 inches long and 3/4 inch wide and has the same swinging heart buttons with inlaid bone as well as a turning rowel. *Ken Miller collection.*

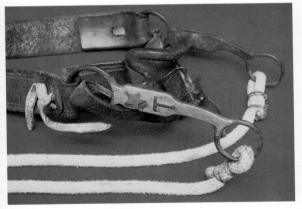

Fred Tucker's personal bit and bridle. *Danielle Hall collection*

WILLIE NATHAN WEAST
1898 - 1965

★★★★★	$$$	◆◆◆◆◆
Collectibility	Value	Scarcity

1898	Born in Mays County, Oklahoma, the third of ten children.
1910	Family moved to Brisco County, Texas.
1917	Willie married Mary Davis.
1918	Parents and some siblings moved to Kansas. Willie worked on local ranches and made bits and spurs.
1930	Had a truck farm, trapped coyotes for bounty, did blacksmithing.
1940s, 1950s	Making bits and spurs full time.
1965	Died in Lockney, TX.

Weast used overlays of silver, brass or copper. He marked his pieces "MADE BY W. WEAST SILVERTON TEX" on the top edge of spurs and outside bit cheek, but occasionally marked just with a W.

Weast marked this spur on the edge of the heel band, MADE BY W.W. WEAST. SILVERTON, TEX. NO. 101.

Occasionally Weast used only a W to identify his work.

Weast marked most pieces in the same manner as J. O. Bass. Frank Loftin collection.

It was rare for a Texas maker to create a loose-jaw bit such as this one. Ray Anderson collection.

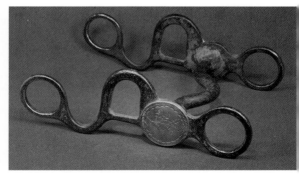

This bit was made for Willie's son, Donald, and is marked D.W. The copper conchos are engraved with an identifiable Weast motif. Doc Wallace collection.

This is an innovative spur design with an unusual chap guard.
Frank Loftin collection.

These spurs are overlaid with brass and silver. Doc Wallace collection

CHARLES H. WYATT
1870 - 1953

★★	$$	◆◆◆◆◆
Collectibility	Value	Scarcity

1870	Born in Powhattan, Kansas.
1885	Grew up helping his blacksmith father.
1898	Moved by wagon to Mesa County, Colorado.
1906	Married Dollie Weyer and lived in Maybell, Colorado.
1916	Elected a Constable in Moffat County.
1926	General blacksmith business and garage in Maybell.
1930s	Worked in copper mines on Douglas Mountain.
1940	Prospecting every summer for silver and gold.
1952	Died peacefully at home in Maybell.

All his pieces were marked with his distinctive logo: a quarter circle over a circle dot. Wyatt made both heavy rodeo-bronc-rider spurs and finely detailed, delicate spurs. He was a skilled blacksmith.

A quarter circle over a circle dot identifies Wyatt's spurs.

Finely detailed plain iron spurs. Dick Robinson collection

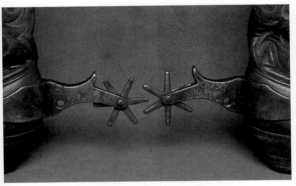

Heavy, bronc-rider spurs made in 1926 for Chuck Roberts. Museum of Northwest Colorado.

HENRY C. ZIMMER
1864 - 1934

★★★	$$$	◆◆◆◆◆
Collectibility	Value	Scarcity

1864	Born in St. Francis County, Missouri.
1866	His mother died.
1878	Father died, leaving him an orphan.
1879	Working in a blacksmith shop in Farmington, MO.
1885	Traveled to California.
1886	Settled in Pecos, Texas, and started blacksmith business.
1891	Married Fannie Mitchell.
1909	Started a hardware business.
1924	Opened an automobile agency.
1929	With son-in-law as a partner, he started the Zimmer-Roddy Motor Co.
1934	Died suddenly of a heart attack.

Zimmer marked his spurs either on the shank or on the heel band.

These iron spurs resemble the O.K. spur that Petmecky and Buermann popularized.
Wheat collection, Ranching Heritage Association, Texas Tech University

Unmarked iron spurs with narrow heelband and small saw-tooth rowels characteristic of Zimmer. Wheat collection.

Other Makers

There are additional makers of Texas-style bits and spurs for whom we have no further information, or marks for which we do not have a maker's name. These are probably all makers of the 20th century, but it is also possible that some of these names could be of the owner of a spur rather than the maker. If anyone knows something about any of these makers, please advise the authors.

T.W. Anderson

Wheat collection, Ranching Heritage Assn., Texas Tech University

Andrews, Joshua, TX

Wheat collection, Ranching Heritage Assn., Texas Tech University

Bob Baldwin

#9647 Canon City Prison, CO. Abe Hays Collection.

J.C. CHAPMAN   *East Texas*

D.M. CLOWER

Lloyd Mitchell Collection.

R.E. COX

Lloyd Mitchell collection.

A.E. DOOLEY, CHEYENNE, WY

Kurt House Collection

FATHEREE

Wheat collection, Ranching Heritage Assn., Texas Tech University

FAY, 101 RANCH

BERNARD FONES

Ken Miller Collection

ERNEST GALLAT

Jay Lyndes Collection

A.D. HALL

Kurt House Collection

MONTE HAY, FREDONIA, TX

KERBY

Wheat collection, Ranching Heritage Assn.,
Texas Tech University

Fabian Klecka 1969

Lloyd Mitchell Collection

Fred Lundie

Abe Hayes Collection

Malcomb

Ed Masell (LEFT SPURS ONLY)

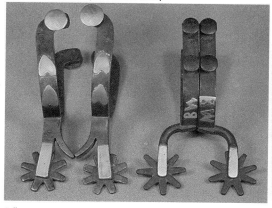

Billy Swope Collection

L. NAIL

Wheat collection, Ranching Heritage Assn., Texas Tech University

POYNER

Frank Loftin Collection

F. ROCHA

Frank Loftin Collection

ROY

Wheat collection, Ranching Heritage Assn., Texas Tech University

RUSSELL

Lloyd Mitchell Collection

SAM

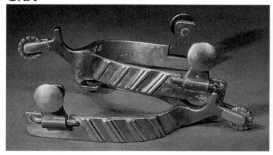

Wheat collection, Ranching Heritage Assn., Texas Tech University

J. SCHELSKE

Larry Peck Collection

SCHRIVER

Panhandle Plains Museum

ELMER SELLERS, FLOYDADA, TX

Wheat collection, Ranching Heritage Assn., Texas Tech University

E.R. Sizer

Governor's Palace, Santa Fe, NM

Sweetwater

Kurt House Collection

A.J.T., Cliff, NM

Bill Chasteen Collection

R.L. TURNER

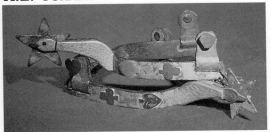

Panhandle Plains Museum

WEATHERBY

Wheat collection, Ranching Heritage Assn., Texas Tech University

WHITE DEER

Bruce Barllett Collection

Glossary

Bit The lower part of a bridle, usually of iron or steel, which is inserted in the mouth of a horse in order to control it.

Bridle The headgear with which a horse is controlled, consisting of a headstall, a bit, reins, and other appendages.

Buttons Small circular ornaments on bits or spurs-usually silver.

Chap guard A small decorative protrusion on the upper side of a spur shank near the connection to the heel band.

Concho In Mexico usually called a *concha* (which translates as shell). A round piece of silver from 1 to 3 inches in diameter, used to ornament bit cheek pieces or spur leathers.

Conquistadores Men who arrived from Spain with Cortez in 1521 to conquer Mexico.

Cricket A round piece of metal with squared edges on the inside where it is mounted on a bar inside the port of a bit. The horse rolls it with his tongue producing the sound of a cricket.

Curb A basic style of bit with a solid mouth piece, some tongue relief, and a strap or chain under the horse's chin.

Double-mounted A spur with embellishment on both sides of the heel band.

Empressario A person who had a land grant in Spanish Texas for the purpose of bringing settlers to work the land and attain ownership.

Half breed A high-port mouthpiece of a bit with a cricket.

Headstall The leather bridle on a horse's head which holds the bit in a horse's mouth. It is attached to the top of a bit.

Heelband The U-shaped portion of a spur which wraps around the heel of a rider's boot.

Inlay To set one material (e.g. silver) into a recessed area in the suface of another (e.g. steel).

Jingle bobs Small ornaments dangling from the center of a spur rowel. They make a pleasing sound with the cadence of a horse's walk. Also known as *pajados*.

Maker's mark The stamp of a maker's name or symbol put on a piece he made.

Monel An alloy of nickel, copper, iron and manganese in certain proportions commonly used to make some bits and spurs in the 1940s and 1950s.

Mounting Embellishment on bit or spur which involves adding silver to the iron or steel form. It may be single or double.

Nickel silver Also known as German silver, it is an alloy of nickel, copper, and tin or zinc. It contains no silver. The first record of its use was in 14th century China as Pakthong. It was perfected in Germany in 1835 as a weapons metal.

Nickel steel An alloy of steel and nickel to achieve the non-corrosive attributes of nickel.

Overlay To lay one metal (e.g. silver) on top of another (e.g. steel) adhered by soldering.

Port A raised, curved piece for a tongue relief in the center of a mouthpiece on a bit.

Rowel The circular piece of metal shaped to create spokes attached to the end of the spur shank with a pin, enabling it to rotate. With the slightest of pressure on a horse's side it encourages the horse to move.

Shank The piece of a spur which is attached to the heel band and to which the rowel is fastened.

Silver, grades of Pure (fine) 99%, sterling 92%, coin 90%.

Single-mounted Spurs with mountings on only one side of the heelband and shank.

Spur A decorative metal implement secured to the heel of a horseman for the purpose of urging movement of his mount by applying pressure to its side.

Spur leather A piece of leather attached to the buttons of a spur to fasten it to a boot.

Stainless steel A steel alloy with 12 to 14% chromium, making it nearly insusceptible to rusting and ordinary corrosion.

Swinging button A hinged piece on the end of a spur heel band to which the leathers are attached.

Tongue relief The raised portion of a mouthpiece which creates space for a horse's tongue.

Vaquero A man who takes care of the cattle. A Mexican word for cowboy.

Wrought iron Iron hammered or beaten into shape with forging tools while it is hot.